WINNING the CULTURE WAR

GOD & COUNTRY
PRESS

WINNING the CULTURE WAR

LINDA RAE HERMANN

DEDICATION

This book is dedicated to the Puritans because they left behind their homeland and entered a fearful wilderness for one reason: They believed God's prophetic decree to establish a new nation for a divine purpose.

ACKNOWLEDGMENTS

I want to acknowledge and thank all my family for their constant support and encouragement for this twenty-year endeavor. I am grateful for my daughter Jessica's help in reading the manuscript from time to time and helping create the Web site. Also, my son, Valentino, has always been sensitive to the Holy Spirit about knowing when to call me and give me words of encouragement. I want to give a big thanks to my forever friends, Sherri, Linda, and Joy, the prayer warriors who prayed this book into being. And of course, and most important, the Lord has been my source of inspiration and understanding since the day in 1989 when He started me on this journey.

CONTENTS

CHAPTER ONE

The Roots of the Culture War

Old Testament History

The children of Israel were encamped near Jericho, preparing to follow God's instructions, assured of victory through obedience. Everything went as planned; they marched for seven days, shouted, and the walls of Jericho fell. However, shortly thereafter, God became angry with an individual's disobedience, and Israel lost a battle with Ai they should have easily won.

Joshua tore his clothes and fell on the ground before the ark, asking God, why this humiliating defeat? The Lord responded, "Get up! Why do you lie thus on your face? Israel has sinned, and they have also transgressed My covenant which I commanded them. For they have even taken some of the accursed things, and have both stolen and deceived; and they have also put *it* among their own stuff" (Josh. 7:10, 11). God went on to reveal that Achan had taken forbidden objects for his personal possession and hidden them in his tent. His disobedience brought a curse on all Israel in the battle of Ai.

Modern History

President Reagan stood in front of the Berlin Wall in 1987 and passionately demanded, "Mr. Gorbachev, tear down this wall!" That cry was wrapped in the power of destiny that continued until it succeeded. In a spiritual sense, the people of the Western world joined in with Reagan's inspirational shout, and in 1989 the wall came down. Miraculously, the Iron Curtain of Soviet Communism and the Berlin Wall fell between 1989 and 1991, after forty years of the Cold War. The people shouted and the wall of Communism fell.

That event was a victory for America and for God, but surprisingly, socialism and its anti-Christian values have become a greater threat now than before the dissolution of the Soviet Union. Even though the Soviet Union fell, it represented only one expression and example of the socialist strategy. Socialist ideas live on throughout the world and in the United States. Anti-Christian, socialist ideas have established and hidden themselves in our national tent. The daily bad news reports indescribable threats to our children, unfathomable, immoral, and criminal acts, the push for abortion and gay marriage, and the government's efforts to redistribute the wealth. All this reveals an ongoing attack on basic Judeo-Christian beliefs of our nation; it's the consequence of Satan's ongoing plan to take God out of our nation.

Satan used the injustices of the Industrial Revolution in the nineteenth century to inspire socialist ideas as a solution. He had laid a foundation of anti-Christian ideas during the Enlightenment and the Romantic Movement of the eighteenth century, creating secular humanism. In the twentieth century, he piled socialist ideas on top of humanism, developing a philosophy and practical strategies that have led to the success of socialists as they replaced our Judeo-Christian principles. Socialist ideas became a force in America in the early part of the twentieth century but reached their peak in the 1960s. It has been unrelenting and increasing ever since. Bill

O'Reilly, author and commentator on Fox News, calls these radical leftists "secular progressives." That term broadens the understanding of socialism because it includes everything secular as well as all anti-God activities.

It's difficult to warn Americans about socialism because the media and educational institutions have reinterpreted it. They make socialism appear harmless and anyone critical of it is made to look foolish and ignorant.

Most people are aware of and even critical of *politically correct* restrictions on our speech, but peer pressure keeps us from speaking the truth and even thinking it. The secular progressives have redefined many words and attached emotional responses to them that block knowledge of the truth. For example, those whose agenda is social change initiated a program for teachers to be *agents of change*. Originally the label *agents of change,* or *change agent,* for teachers meant they were to see themselves as agents who changed the social structure of society rather than teachers of important knowledge. When I mentioned agents of change in a critical manner to a friend, she said that change agents could be a good thing. It's obvious that a good spin has been put on that phrase that will make it difficult to expose the conspiracy behind its formulation. The manipulation of the public is approaching a high level of precision.

Another example of conditioning is the response to Miss California Carrie Prejean's answer to a question at the Miss USA contest. She was asked about homosexual marriage, and she stated that she believed marriage should be between a man and a woman. The reaction of the secular left was immediate and punishing. It's obvious that that definition of marriage is being colored with negative emotions, making people feel they're intolerant and hard-hearted if they hold to the belief that marriage is for one man and one woman. The traditional definition of marriage will continue to be maligned until the general public turns from its fear of speaking out against homosexual marriage.

If someone mentions socialism in mixed company, as if it's a threat, the psychological conditioning of most Americans has made them feel that anyone who criticizes socialism or leftist ideas is out of touch with the real world. Ongoing manipulation from the media and educational centers has made people feel that socialism is ancient history, not to be taken seriously, and that anyone who thinks it's a threat is a kook.

The general feeling of the public, even pastors and other Christian leaders, is the desire to distance themselves from anyone identifying socialism as a real threat. They don't want to appear foolish and ignorant.

Liberal Manipulation

In fact, the emotions most often manipulated are those that can make people feel insensitive, bigoted, and/or foolish and ignorant. The manipulation all plays upon a person's sense of pride, wanting to appear to be a good or at least an intelligent person. For example, Prejean was made to look like a *bad* person—insensitive and bigoted. The same is true of former president Bush and Sarah Palin—they've been made continually to look foolish. Of course, ridicule is a favorite weapon of liberals.

Socialist Strategy

Why is socialism a threat to Judeo-Christian America? We may have defeated the political and national arm of Communism in the Soviet Union by winning the Cold War, but the real threat of revolution has always been from within, not without. Not all socialist ideas are evil and strike out against God. The original ideas of utopian socialists were not a threat to the social, cultural, and political identity of a nation. Robert Owen in England and Francois Marie Charles Fourier in France were seeking a solution for the unjust labor practices of the Industrial Revolution. They didn't press for social change, revolutionizing cultures and economies by a complete remaking of society. In fact, the United States has even adopted some socialist innovations, such as progressive taxes, regulation of business, Medicare, social security, and financial help for the poorest in our society. However, there is a form of socialism, the more radical Marxist kind, that has connected social change with economic change. Liberals have been working from within our society and within influential institutions to prepare the way for a more fundamental change in our government and economy that will lead to the eventual loss of our human rights and democratic institutions. These liberal progressives have already succeeded in our culture by replacing most of our Judeo-Christian principles with secular ones.

This radical brand of socialism is what concerns us. These socialistic ideas are promoting fundamental and revolutionary social change that supports the goal of replacing capitalism with socialism. Whether it's called socialism or communism doesn't matter; time has reinterpreted their meanings, but in the end, certain basic principles and strategies flow from one philosophical source. For our purposes, they are one and the same, and *socialism shall be the primary term to identify the adversary that has worn away the Judeo-Christian composition of our nation.*

As socialism has developed its strategies and methods for revolution throughout the twentieth and twenty-first centuries, it has become an umbrella that united many anti-Christian opponents working to make America a secular nation: secular humanists, atheists, anarchists, heretics, and secular progressives. God and His church have had many enemies in recent times, but the socialists have been the most insidious and successful in infiltrating our institutions—churches, education, media, government, political parties, courts—and over time using these institutions to replace the Judeo-Christian values with secular/socialist ones. J. Edgar Hoover, former director of the FBI, warned of this plan in his book, *Masters of Deceit,* stating that the strategies of Lenin and Stalin were to infiltrate American institutions. He quoted their plan:

> This was precisely the tactic of "infiltration" advocated by Lenin and Stalin. As Communist International General Secretary Georgi Dimitroff told the Seventh World Congress of the Comintern in 1935: "Comrades, you remember the ancient tale of the capture of Troy. Troy was inaccessible to the armies attacking her, thanks to her impregnable walls. And the attacking army, after suffering many sacrifices, was unable to achieve

victory until, with the aid of the famous Trojan horse, it managed to penetrate to the very heart of the enemy's camp."[1]

The infiltrating socialists were not in a hurry, and they had many soldiers. One plan was developed by communists in the Soviet Union who created guidelines for spreading socialism through a violent overthrow of governments or by infiltrating mainstream institutions in order to manipulate the values of a society while revolutionizing them from within.

The second plan was formulated by Saul Alinsky, a community organizer and Marxist from Chicago. He developed very effective methods and tactics; ones that when studied and applied became powerful tools for socialists, activists, and secular progressives from the 1960s to the present.

Soviet-Influenced Goals

The Communist Revolution in Russia in 1917 began nearly a century of threat from Soviet socialism that eventually became the Cold War after World War II. Our concern, however, is to see how the socialist ideas have infiltrated our nation and revolutionized our culture. In 1958, Cleon Skousen, author of *The Naked Communist,* described forty-five socialist goals and strategies, warning Americans of a communist campaign "to soften America for the final takeover." Skousen used the terminology of the time to describe the Soviet Union. He used the word *communism* more than *socialism* because the Soviet Union referred to itself as "Communist," although their initials, USSR, stood for the Union of Soviet Socialist Republics. Please note that any reference to communism in this book is a reference to socialism. Skousen drew these goals from socialist literature and congressional reports. He summarized them in 1958. In addition, on January 10, 1963, a list of forty-five communist goals were entered into the *Congressional Record* by Representative A. S. Herlong Jr. of Florida. The following twenty-six goals are the ones that have been used most successfully by socialists and other radicals to revolutionize our culture and initiate the Culture War. They reveal how the revolutionary ideas—the accursed things—were planted in our culture:

1. Capture one or both of the political parties in the United States.
2. Use technical decisions of the courts to weaken basic American institutions by claiming their activities violate civil rights.
3. Get control of the schools. Use them as transmission belts for socialism and current Communist propaganda. Soften the curriculum. Get control of teachers' associations. Put the party line in textbooks.
4. Gain control of all student newspapers.
5. Use student riots to foment public protests against programs or organizations which are under Communist attack.
6. Infiltrate the press. Get control of book-review assignments, editorial writing, and policy-making positions.
7. Gain control of key positions in radio, TV, and motion pictures.
8. Continue discrediting American culture by degrading all forms of artistic expression. An American Communist cell was told to "eliminate all good sculpture from parks and buildings, substitute shapeless, awkward, and meaningless forms."
9. Control art critics and directors of art museums. 'Our plan is to promote ugliness, repulsive, meaningless art.'
10. Eliminate all laws governing obscenity by calling them 'censorship' and a violation of free speech and free press.
11. Break down cultural standards of morality by promoting pornography and obscenity in books, magazines, motion pictures, radio, and TV.
12. Present homosexuality, degeneracy, and promiscuity as 'normal, natural, healthy.'
13. Infiltrate the churches and replace revealed religion with 'social' religion. Discredit the Bible and emphasize

the need for intellectual maturity, which doesn't need a 'religious crutch.'

14. Eliminate prayer or any phase of religious expression in the schools on the ground that it violates the principle of "separation of church and state."

15. Discredit the American Constitution by calling it inadequate, old-fashioned, out of step with modern needs, a hindrance to cooperation between nations on a worldwide basis.

16. Discredit the American Founding Fathers. Present them as selfish aristocrats who had no concern for the 'common man.'

17. Belittle all forms of American culture and discourage the teaching of American history on the ground that it was only a minor part of the 'big picture.' Give more emphasis to Russian history since the Communists took over.

18. Support any socialist movement to give centralized control over any part of the culture—education, social agencies, welfare programs, mental health clinics, etc.

19. Eliminate the House Committee on Un-American Activities.

20. Discredit and eventually dismantle the FBI.

21. Infiltrate and gain control of more unions.

22. Infiltrate and gain control of big business. (Not as successful as some of the others)

23. Transfer some of the powers of arrest from the police to social agencies. Treat all behavioral problems as psychiatric disorders which no one but psychiatrists can understand [or treat].

24. Discredit the family as an institution. Encourage promiscuity and easy divorce.

25. Emphasize the need to raise children away from the negative influence of parents. Attribute prejudices, mental blocks, and retarding of children to suppressive influence of parents.

26. Create the impression that violence and insurrection are legitimate aspects of the American tradition; that students and special-interest groups should rise up and use ["]united force["] to solve economic, political or social problems.[2]

This is not a recent list someone is trying to pass off as having been fashioned in the 1950s. It was published in the book, *The Naked Communist,* in 1958 and entered into the *Congressional Record* in 1963. It's hard to believe we were clearly warned early on and didn't take the warning seriously. What is shocking about this list is the fact that almost all of the twenty-six goals have been implemented with a great deal of success. Besides guidelines for social change, such as undermining the family; discrediting the Founding Fathers and the Constitution; removing prayer from schools; promoting student unrest, homosexuality, and pornography; and undermining parental rights, the list also points out some of the institutions that were targeted for takeover, such as the political parties, courts, schools, unions, news and entertainment media, big business, political parties, family, churches, and the arts. Socialists designed a plan to take control of the American's culture, society, and the economy by infiltrating its institutions. They hid away their ideas, the *accursed objects* mentioned above, in the most influential institutions in our society that would bring about radical social change. They knew that by taking over these institutions, enabling them to work from within, they could revolutionize the culture, even if they could not overthrow our government or capitalist system from without. These social changes would open the door to the economic, revolutionary goals of socialism.

Review of Some of the Socialist Successes

The first goal on the list above is the takeover of one or both of the political parties. When did that happen? "I didn't leave the Democratic Party. It left me," declared Ronald Reagan in 1962 when he changed parties. He had been a Democrat during the New Deal, but became disillusioned by the gradual dominance of the far left in the party. Although the Democratic Party has always retained some traditional members, the Left clinched power in the party after President Kennedy's assassination in 1963 when Lyndon Johnson began his agenda for the Great Society and then his War on Poverty in 1964. Liberals had been making headway to control the party since the New Deal, but it was under President Johnson they were able to solidify their power. Socialists infiltrated the programs of the War on Poverty[3] and welfare, and government spending increased exponentially during those years. The main role of government became the caretaking of the poor, and the only morality that mattered was helping the poor and underprivileged. Other moral issues were set aside in order to pursue this one purpose and free Americans from the capitalistic superstructure.

The movements at the end of the 1960s entrenched this more socialistic, liberal idea in the Democratic Party that made them focus on turning corporation to the left until recently. It continued to stay left until the Republican Congress and President Clinton agreed to reform the welfare system in the 1990s. Clinton was a realist and tried to move the party to the middle. Since then the Democratic Party has been under pressure to move away from its far left wing, but with the election of Barack Obama, it's clear the party is presently moving headlong to the Left.

Others socialist successes followed the upheavals of the 1960s. Roe v. Wade in 1973 and many cases that followed reveal the success of the second goal. At that time, the majority of citizens didn't support making abortion legal. The Left used the courts to gain their goals. Overreaching into the separate powers of the legislative branch, the courts began to legislate secular ideas, forcing them onto an unwilling American public. Then the takeover of the public school system through the teachers' unions and progressive educators provided one more institution to promote secular, progressive ideas. This plan had been in the works since the early 1900s. Liberal professors of education taught teachers to become agents of change in their classroom. The majority of professors in colleges and universities were and still are secular progressives, spinning their opinions as if they were facts. As propaganda and brainwashing furiously increased in the educational field, at the same time, they spread through the media—the movies, television, and the news media. The infiltration was successful because educated liberal elites extended their dominance in all the institutions that had the most influence over the minds of Americans. Since the transformation of these institutions, winning the Culture War has been an uphill fight and, at times, has felt hopeless.

In this book, I will draw upon many of my own personal experiences to illustrate the ideas I am presenting. I walked on the edges and sometimes in the middle of the Cultural Revolution, which began in the 1960s. In many ways, I feel like Hosea, who had to live what he wrote. Even if I was not always in God's will, God has used my experiences to help me understand the Enemy's plans and activities.

Historical Illustration Drawn from My Life

We moved into our new apartment, or "pad," as it was referred to in those days, about ten of us—my husband and I and eight other hippies. We had come upon a larger place where we could live together. My husband and I were in our late twenties, and our roommates were teenagers. We had found them on the streets without a place to crash and took them home, but our place was too small. So, here we were in our new apartment, living with eight teenagers who had turned away from their middle-class roots. That was normal for Haight-Ashbury in the Summer of Love, 1967.

Food was free, one meal a day in the park. Clothes were free at the Free Store. You could "crash" with anyone who had a pad. It was all socialist inspired: "From each according to his faculties, to each according to his needs!" We didn't know the philosophy behind our actions, but that didn't stop us from following it. Of course, other aspects of socialism manifested themselves as well. Traditional morality and religion and the traditional family were capitalist ploys to control and oppress the masses, so free love replaced moral restrictions. Our goal was to strip society of its Puritan inhibitions.

One of the girls living with us completely lost her sense of dignity and self-respect, convinced that free love was part of the new culture. Through drug use and mental confusion, she slipped over the edge into complete promiscuity, disappearing after a few days of giving herself over to every man who wanted her. The seeds of destruction for the hippie culture were visible even in the beginning of the summer. By the time we left to go to New York in the middle of the summer, everything had fallen apart: Violence had erupted; hardcore drug dealers took over the drug scene, killing hippie dealers; pimps went in search of new prostitutes; young people overdosed daily; and the free food disappeared.

Many people laugh at the hippie movement, but it was used to entice people across the nation to throw off our Judeo-Christian heritage. Not because people wanted to be communists, but because people wanted to be free from moral restrictions. They wanted to "Do their own thing" and follow their lusts. The popular saying was, "If it feels good, do it." The 1960s may seem like ancient history; however, those ideas remain in the consciousness of our nation. They help to form our ideas and transform the institutions of religion, family, the courts, the universities, unions, the media, and government. These are some of the trappings of socialism that remain in the American tent.

The hippie movement and the student unrest of the 1960s could be seen as a volcano that had threatened eruption for years. The internal workings of socialist infiltrators had been applying pressure by practicing the goals above. Now their ideas and values erupted and overflowed with fire for a radical change throughout society. Over the next forty years, the lava of change spread into the mainstream until the socialist, secular revolution was established in the major institutions and thought-life of our society.

Saul Alinsky's Plan and Tactics

Exclusive: Self-proclaimed bible [sic] thumper Miss California, Carrie Prejean, should start pointing the finger at herself for her own indiscretions. TheDirty.com has received exclusive images of the homophobic debutante that would clearly strip her of her Miss California crown. So much for being a good role model for the state of California Carrie. Looks like your Dirty photo shoot makes you a sinner too.[4]

The above quote from *thedirty.com* Web site attacks Miss California 2009, Carrie Prejean, for stating her belief that marriage should be between a man and a woman. It's a perfect example of one of the tactics developed by Saul Alinsky. It's rule number four: "Make the enemy live up to their own book of rules."[5]

Once Prejean expressed her opinion and related it to her Christian faith, the news media went searching for some actions in her past that violated her Christian beliefs. They found risqué photos taken in two circumstances as part of her modeling career and used those to condemn her. At the time of those photo shoots, it probably seemed harmless to her since her own moral boundaries had already been compromised by the modeling industry. All Christians have to struggle to find their way on their journey, and many make some poor decisions while they are first learning how to apply God's principles to their lives. God is gracious and gives us the opportunity to grow and improve without condemning us, but the liberal news media is not a merciful god. Many of its disciples have their nit-picking agenda, and there is no room for grace when it comes to Christians or conservatives.

The liberal press learned its techniques from the socialist and Chicago community organizer, Saul Alinsky, who had influence and success far beyond any recognition or fame. His book, *Rules for Radicals*, was a handbook that taught a stealth method of transforming the culture. "But Alinsky's brand of revolution was not characterized by dramatic, sweeping, overnight transformations of social institutions. As Richard Poe puts it, "Alinsky viewed revolution as a slow, patient process. The trick was to penetrate existing institutions such as churches, unions and political parties. He advised organizers and their disciples to quietly, subtly gain influence within the decision-making ranks of these institutions, and to introduce changes from that platform."[6] The connection between the socialist goals that were entered into the *Congressional Record* and those of Alinsky is very apparent. Obviously, socialists didn't operate in a vacuum but read and discussed ways to make the revolution happen within and through the institutions of American society. As one reads the chapter on tactics in *Rules for Radicals,* the methods and tactics to obtain those goals become clear. Although Alinsky is only one of many voices for socialism, studying his methods helps us understand the general approach used to achieve the socialist goal to remake society and redistribute the wealth.

Chapter seven will go in depth to describe Alinsky's plan and tactics. It will also present methods to disarm those tactics. There are ways to win in an encounter with those trained in Alinsky's tactics. It takes practice, prayer, godly shrewdness, and wisdom. For example, Carrie Prejean could have avoided the attack by answering the question if homosexuals should be able to marry by saying, "The majority of Californians just voted for a constitutional amendment to define marriage as between a man and a woman. I have been raised in a traditional home, so I agree with the majority of Californians." Or she could have said after all the attacks, "I don't understand why I have been so harshly criticized. The majority of Californians believe the same way I do. They voted to amend the constitution to keep marriage between a man and a woman." Just by relating her views to the majority would have made it difficult for her critics to declare her out of step with the state she represented as Miss California. Besides, any criticism of Prejean's belief and opinion would be a criticism of the majority of Californians.

Teaching Christians how to disarm the weapons of Alinsky's disciples is a major goal of this book. Although he died in 1972, his disciples continue to use his methods and strategy to remake the culture and make their critics ineffective and powerless. President Obama and Hillary Clinton are two of his important disciples. They were greatly influenced by him and derived many of their tactics from him—Hillary wrote her BA honors thesis about Alinsky, and Obama studied under Alinsky's disciples in Chicago. Even though that knowledge gives us greater insight into both politicians, it's not a focus of this book. Rather, our goal is to uncover the way the secular progressives, or socialists, have stripped our culture of its

Judeo-Christian heritage and to design a plan to restore that godly heritage.

Our Adversaries

The last forty years have revealed the wiliness and determination of our opponents. It will be no easy task to defeat them, but with more knowledge of our adversaries and the guidance of the Holy Spirit, we should be able to reverse their successes. Also on our side is the fact that there are not many idealists in the upper levels of power because most ideologues are no longer motivated by their ideology after they move into positions of power. They have had to sacrifice their integrity so many times to achieve their ends that any remaining idealism is unlikely. Although some have been sucked into a socialist mindset without understanding the philosophical underpinnings of their beliefs, others have hardened over time and go through the motions of idealism. The Clintons and their entourage are examples of those who lost their vision and sacrificed what they originally saw as a virtuous end goal, because they practiced unethical means to obtain it.

Then there are the few and the most threatening secular progressives: those who have retained their personal character and faith in the cause during the climb to power. They are the ones who have achieved power while still being true believers. These true believers not only have political power but also have power through their character because they are not hardened and therefore live according to their beliefs. That is the difference between Bill and Hillary Clinton and Barack Obama. The Clintons began as believers but ended as players, while Obama received power before having sold his soul and losing his idealism and faith. He is a true believer, and that is why we are seeing early in his presidency the power and influence he has over people. His character, while it doesn't line up with God's standard, does line up with what he believes to be right and just. He is not a phony or a hypocrite, and that is what makes him a very strong opponent in the Culture War. Therefore, it will take totally committed Christians with strong Christian character and godly shrewdness to save our culture and society from the century-old goals and efforts of socialists.

Conspiracies Do Happen

When we think of conspiracies, we picture people sitting down at a table and developing a strategy. That is too simplistic when a movement lasts for many centuries. Although there is always an elite group of thinkers who present radical and revolutionary ideas, it's not usually controlled from the top by a strict formula. However, in the case of Soviet Communism, its leaders did construct a plan in the first part of the twentieth century. In the early and mid-twentieth century, the more extreme socialists—governments and ideologues—conspired to spread socialism throughout the world. Their plan continues to be relevant because it was well defined and it worked, providing a method to other anti-Judeo-Christian activists who adopted those methods. Humanists and progressives blended in with socialists to take on new names, but they had the same goals. There have always been humanists or secularists in America who have made efforts to replace its Judeo-Christian foundation with a more secular one. The socialist plan provided new directions, methods, and guidelines to this group, and it became the means of success for the Cultural Revolution and the Culture War.

At the present, it appears that the socialists and secularists have succeeded in replacing with secular ones the Judeo-Christian principles on which our nation is built. Sexual freedom, abortion, nontraditional family, activist judges, dominant central government, moral relativism, and the redefinition of marriage are only a few of the revolutionary changes of our culture. The majority have accepted secular practices and ideas. It doesn't mean the majority of our citizens are socialists; many don't even know what socialism is. However, it does mean that they have gone along with the secularization of our society. Even many Christians practice secular morality and vote for politicians who don't agree with their Christian beliefs. Numerous Christians practice a very shallow faith. They have been enticed with secular ideas about sex, family, marriage, and government's role because of the brainwashing by the public education system and the liberal media, and also because it allows self-gratification instead of self-denial.

Even though most Americans would never think of themselves as socialists or secular progressives, many think and act like them. The next section will show how socialist ideas have infiltrated our society and economy. As mentioned above, they initiated social changes and economic changes. In fact, the social changes were the means to accomplish the end of economic change. For many Christians, the social changes have been the most alarming. Those changes promoted immoral and unethical beliefs and behavior that opposed the foundational moral principles and the purpose of our nation. It has brought many of our citizens to uncivilized, brutish, and immoral behavior that is a great distress to many dedicated Christians. It's also very distressing to the Lord because He has called our nation to a more holy vocation.

Although the social changes are alarming to Christians, the economic changes are also a threat. The economic aspects of socialism revolutionize our constitution, government, and the political principles upon which our political system is based. Both the social and economic changes need to be seen as enemies of the Lord and His goals. Understanding socialist ideas, strategies, and goals will help the reader understand how our society has been revolutionized and how we can undo their successes.

Socialist Ideology

It's important to understand why socialism is a threat so we can know how to reverse its inroads into American culture and government. Socialists associate capitalism with Christianity, traditional values, and traditional institutions. Marxist socialists presented the view that those who possessed economic power created institutional structures in society, such as government, religion, family, and morality, in order to perpetuate the economic system that benefited them. According to socialists in America, the main economic system was the oppressive capitalism, or the free market. They believed that different institutions, traditions, and ideas were created to support, strengthen, and preserve capitalism that in turn oppressed the have-nots, or the poorest. The Constitution, checks and balances of the three branches of government, the arts, news and entertainment media, churches, Judeo-Christian values, the traditional family, absolute morality, faith in God, and education were all instituted to support capitalism. Therefore in order to overthrow capitalism, they had to destroy the institutional structures and traditional values that to Marxists supported the capitalist economic system.

One could describe the socialist worldview through the following analogy: To the socialists, capitalism was like a house. The foundation consisted of the basic principles and values of the capitalist society: free market, privately owned means of production, and limited regulation of corporations. Every post, beam, and panel stood for the different institutions that supported and framed the house. These institutions are the ones mentioned above, having to do with education, media, arts, business, government, and church or religion, the "opiate" of the people. To the socialists or secular progressives, America was a capitalist house or economic system built upon a capitalist foundation. Capitalist principles fed into all of the posts, panels, and beams—the movies, arts, education, media, etc.—determining the kind of house that was built. The institutions were used and manipulated by capitalists to build and preserve the house.

American socialists believed that the have-nots were weighted down under the foundation. The house of capitalism was built on the backs of the lower class, or proletariat. In order to free and prosper the Have-nots, the interior support structures had to be replaced with new ones. Each institution had to be reformed to support socialist ideas. They had to attack the foundation and infiltrate the supporting posts and beams, the societal institutions, and use them to replace the capitalist foundation with socialist principles. If they revolutionized the structure from within, people would not know it was a new house until it was too late. That is the strategy that has transformed our society and culture from one based upon Judeo-Christian principles to one based upon secular-socialist principles.

The above analogy can also be used to explain and describe American society and culture as God intended them. Although never perfect, God had a building, or nation, in mind when He sent the Pilgrims and Puritans to lay the foundation for our national house. The Puritans laid the foundation of Judeo-Christian principles from which the rest of the structures drew their purpose. The posts and beams—churches, schools, government, family, business, newspapers, arts—all became the means to build the American house after God's design. The economic system, which from the beginning had capitalist aspects, was only one post or a beam, not the foundation. The Christian principles of being responsible, having self-control, working hard, and being industrious supported an open attitude to the capitalism that arose in later centuries. However, God's insistence that Christians take care of the poor, orphan, and widow just as readily supported a willingness to restrict injustices resulting from capitalism.

The house that God built had a special purpose. He built it upon a "hill" for the world to see. God wanted His American house to be a light, reflecting His character. Whenever it fell into darkness, God called His prophets to preach a message of repentance, restoring the nation to justice. For example, when Great Britain and the King ignored the rights of the colonists, God declared and established the rights of man through Thomas Jefferson and his compatriots. When the South would not give up slavery, God called his abolitionist prophets to bring repentance and justice. When blacks in the South were denied equal rights, God called his prophets, Martin Luther King, Jr. and his fellow organizers, to institute justice. God's house has not been perfect, but it has always been seeking perfection.

The socialists and secularists are wrong about America. It has always been a nation on the road to justice, and its inspiration comes from its roots, its Judeo-Christian foundation. Replacing its foundation, its posts, and its beams with man-made principles and righteousness can only end in disaster. They are false prophets, and they shall not prevail. We must prevail, but we have to do some soul searching and repentance; we have to find God's mind and strategy for restoration; we have to become shrewd but innocent in using tactics to reestablish our Judeo-Christian foundation; we have to rebuild our house from within.

Further Explanation of Socialism

The following examples give more insight into how and why socialists dismantled our traditional American house. Socialists saw churches or religion as used to protect the economic system that benefited the middle and upper classes (the bourgeoisie) and keep the lower class (the proletariat) at the bottom. To socialists, Christianity is and was part of the superstructure that supported the system that degraded and oppressed the poorest in society—the have-nots. For that reason, their present-day descendants—secular progressives or liberals—continue to strive to remove Christianity and God from our institutions and government. The attack on prayer in schools, the attack on God in our swearing-in ceremonies, and the assault on our money are just a few examples of the secular goals.

Christianity was also a focus of the onslaught from socialists because socialist and humanist philosophy is based upon the belief that man doesn't possess a soul or spirit, but is strictly matter. The socialists' idea is that man is derived from matter—evolution—and is limited to being matter. Since human beings are the highest animal in the animal kingdom, their animal nature need not be restrained except where it leads to violence or disruption of order. Humankind's animal nature, which is basically good, can be controlled by providing economic equality, doing away with envy and competition, and consequently removing the motive for evil.

As a result of this unrealistic thinking, Communists and socialists thought they could provide the means for people to be good; therefore, religion was not necessary to retain order and avoid lawlessness. Moral principles involving sexuality, character development, and natural inclinations were not necessary, because unnatural desires were not a violation of moral laws since moral laws didn't exist. By removing moral absolutes, socialists provided a motivation for people to accept the socialist-secular system since it allowed them to pursue personal inclinations and free love without condemnation.

The socialists attack on the traditional family is harder to understand. If there are more single-parent families, more children would be in poverty, which is the opposite of socialists' goals—helping the have-nots get out of poverty. However, if family is redefined and it removes fathers from the home, since the mom is usually the one parent, then more families will be in poverty and will have to depend upon the government for survival. One-parent families will support socialism because they need help financially and emotionally. Also, without the traditional definition of family, gays can become parents, and this will assure their support of socialism because they want to redefine marriage and family to fit their desires. Therefore, socialists and the Left gained support by undermining traditional institutions.

Nontraditional families also provide a psychological benefit for the Left. Children without fathers are more unstable and vulnerable to manipulation by a caretaking government or charismatic leader. Since God created every child with an internal need for a loving father, children without fathers possess an empty place in their heart that needs to be filled. They will seek fulfillment one way or another. In other words, redefining the traditional family—removing the father—creates vulnerable children looking for a father figure to feel whole. Therefore, the socialists make sure the people are broken, and then they obtain the loyalty of those broken people by meeting their physical and emotional needs. Their methods create a cult mentality.

Personal Experience

My parents took my sister and me away from our extended family and moved to California. I was just entering first grade. I only saw my relatives a few times as I grew up. Both my parents worked throughout the years, and I was left alone often. I had some close moments with my mother at times, but I had very little relationship with my father. He was very pleasant but at the same time very quiet. I didn't know I was missing anything; I just accepted my life as normal.

As a result of their neglect and absence, I grew up thinking I was a very strong and independent person. I appeared to be confident and very much of a leader. I was president of my sophomore class, a cheerleader in my junior year, and ASB president in my senior year. I was outgoing and people liked me.

When I went off to college, I had the plan for my life and I began to pursue it. Then my parents got a divorce and both remarried soon after to people who didn't welcome their children. Their divorce and remarriages stirred up in me previously unknown feelings of loneliness and emptiness. It was then I began to seek to fill those empty places.

I entered a convent for two years in search of family relationships. On leaving the convent, I gravitated to the hippie movement in San Francisco, again looking for family. I met and fell in love with an artist and we married. We moved to the country as did many hippies. We moved up to Humboldt County in northern California. It was there I began to search again for something that I felt was missing. I accepted the Lord at a camp when I was twelve years old, so I was also searching for Christian fellowship. I was drawn to a Christian man and his wife who owned a small five-and-dime store. They invited my husband and me to their home, and we joined their fellowship.

The fellowship satisfied some of my continued hunger for family, but a danger lurked in this family. The pastor was a self-made pastor; he had no previous seminary training. He was charismatic and played on his charisma to create a following. It was during the Jesus Movement of the 1970s, and there were many such self-made leaders. Many of them, like Jim Jones, were actually cult leaders. This pastor had some of these cult powers and characteristics. Since I had never had a relationship with my father, I found myself falling under his control. My need for a father surfaced and made me vulnerable to a deceptive leader.

I am grateful to the Lord for warning me at that time and working with me to pull away from the power this pastor had over me. This story is a good example of how a dysfunctional, fatherless family can make people unstable. My need blinded me for a time to the deceptive devices this man used to try to control me. Most of the other people in this fellowship had the same background as I did. They had weak or no relationships with their fathers. In fact, during the hippie movement, many people were vulnerable to deceivers and cult leaders for that reason.

Presently, there are many more fatherless families than during the sixties and seventies. The danger is much greater and our nation more vulnerable to a political leader who could use the need for a father to make himself a demagogue and an idol.

Economic Socialism

The twenty-six goals above have had great success in changing our culture. The effect of the social changes on our society and their threat to our Judeo-Christian principles are obvious, but the socialist economic changes are just as anti-God and anti-Christian as the social changes. Why are the economic goals of socialism a threat to America?

Earlier we showed in the analogy of the house that God had a specific plan for how the American house was built. Judeo-Christian principles formed the foundation, and these principles guided the other institutions. The economic post of the structure was only one aspect of the house. God would have it be in harmony with His principles, but it didn't dominate the house. As mentioned above, when the free market principles were in conflict with Judeo-Christian principles, movements arose to correct injustices. Another example occurred in the early twentieth century in America. Many pastors and church leaders developed a social gospel to bring Christian principles into the marketplace. Its advocates related Christian ideas with the immediate need to help those caught in an unjust economic system. In spite of Christian-inspired reforms, socialists were never content with these economic reforms because they didn't lead to a socialist economic system.

The final goal of socialism is economic. The other changes to society are for the purpose of creating a socialist economy. What is that kind of economy? The extreme form is government ownership of all means of production. In other words, government would own industries, such as banks, automobile manufacturers, the transportation systems, health industries, etc. People could not own their own businesses or homes, and they would work for the state. The government would determine how much would be supplied to consumers—a planned economy—rather than the free market and supply and demand.

Since the fall of the Soviet Union, a total planned economy idea has gone out of favor. The form of socialism more familiar to the West concentrates on redistributing the wealth by using taxes and some government ownership or control. Industries, business, and the richest pay a much higher tax so the government can redistribute wealth to the poorest. Most western economies, including the United States, have some mixture of capitalism and socialism. Our income tax system is progressive, meaning the more you make the greater the portion you pay. As mentioned earlier, our government regulates industries and corporations more or less depending upon the times and the laws. Our tax system increases and decreases its tax on the wealthiest depending upon which party is in power and the economic needs of a particular time. Still, America has a definite preference for the free market and capitalism.

If socialism increasingly replaces capitalism, it would result in greater dependence on government. Government-run health care is the recent effort that could give the government, especially the executive branch, excessive power in the medical field. Government jobs would increase and people's dependence on government would hold back people's willingness to limit its power. Another fear is: What is next? Will the central government take over the education system that is presently part of states' rights and responsibilities? If so, it would weaken the states' ability to check the federal government. In addition, federally run schools would provide a unified curriculum that could be used to support socialist, liberal ideas. In other words, the government would become so powerful, and the people would become so dependent upon it, that it would violate the principles upon which our nation is founded.

Our constitution would no longer be the supreme law of the land, guiding all other laws. We would have to redefine the powers of the different branches of government to accommodate their new roles in running the economy, and they would no longer provide checks and balances on each other. Most power would then rest in the executive branch—the president. Our government would no longer follow the form created by our Founding Fathers.

Our Founding Fathers set up the three branches with separate powers—checks and balances—in order to avoid ultimate power in any one branch or person. Our founders knew that men were not angels, which is a Christian idea based upon the understanding of original sin. Therefore, they formed a government with internal checks and balances. They made the Constitution the Supreme Law of the United States of America, rather than giving that power to any one branch of government. Socialism would undo that arrangement and place too much power in the hands of a few.

The Declaration of Independence states, "We hold these truths to be self-evident, that all men are created equal, that they are endowed by their Creator with certain unalienable rights, that among these are Life, Liberty and the pursuit of Happiness." The few, some branch of government, or the president is not the source of our rights. Our right to life, liberty, and pursuing happiness rests in God, the Creator. If citizens don't know the source of their rights, they will entrust them to government. The government or president would naturally appear to be the preserver and source of human rights. They would be given the power to gives us our rights and take them away. Losing our rights is actually not something that may happen in the future. Since Roe v. Wade, babies in the womb have been denied their right to life because women can terminate their pregnancy for any reason. Now, added to having abortions for personal reasons, it's the practice of using ultrasound to see if the baby has any defects. If some disability is found, such as Down syndrome, the parents are pressured to terminate the pregnancy. We are not talking about a future loss of rights—we have already lost some.

With socialism, the government replaces God and determines our rights. It provides the economic needs of the people, and the people surrender their rights to the government. The Declaration of Independence becomes a false front for hiding the truth. It's extolled as our ideal but without any substance. It's a means to deceive the people that they have rights when they don't. If we continue to allow our culture and society to be ruled by socialist and secular ideals, we will lose all our freedom. We will be a shell of the glorious plan God initiated through His heroic Pilgrim and Puritan Warriors. They were Culture Warriors who established a new nation and a new culture in order provide a haven for the world's poorest and to expand justice and freedom to nations throughout the world whose masses had no rights or hope.

The Solution to the Socialist Plan

We know that socialists formulated a plan to infiltrate American institutions and revolutionize American values in the early twentieth century. Their goals were entered into the *Congressional Record* in 1962. Socialists or liberals have followed those goals and accomplished them. Saul Alinsky developed *Rules for Radicals* that have been used successfully to also help achieve socialist objectives. They have learned how to pressure individuals, groups, and institutions to bend to their will through ridicule and shame. Alinsky created tactics that have been used with great success.

What will it take to reverse their strategy? Christians will have to reenter the institutions presently controlled by liberals and restore Judeo-Christian principles to their visions and mission statements as well as to their decision-making processes. Christians will have to reenter the marketplace of ideas, not only the marketplace of money. The churches or the Internet will have to become the training ground (the boot camps) for producing what Bill O'Reilly calls Culture Warriors. Churches do have the responsibility to bring people to salvation. disciple them, and develop new spiritual leaders. Yet, there is one more responsibility: to train the majority of Christians to impact their communities and restore and maintain Judeo-Christian principles in society and culture, especially in America. These warriors will not only need practical and spiritual training but also follow-up support for years. The mission field is filled with mines, and it will take a well-mapped-out plan to avoid the mines and successfully outwit the enemy.

The next chapter reveals the great importance our mission has. America has a unique calling and therefore, our churches have an added responsibility to fulfill God's plan for our nation. However, if churches don't respond, then future Culture Warriors should go online to receive training from our Web site. Chapters two through five will explain and describe America's ongoing calling and its successes. Then the plan for Christians to become agents of restoration will begin in chapter six.

Call to Action

The time has come to follow God's way for calling more believers into action for the restoration of our culture. Just as David had to find God's prescribed way to bring back the Ark of the Covenant in 1 Chronicles 13 and 15, so too we need to find God's prescribed way as agents of restoration. We have been unsuccessful only because we have not yet learned God's method to win the Culture War. Let us follow long-proven methods that God has repeatedly used to achieve His goals. Let us follow the way of making a covenant with our hearts and minds as did our Puritan ancestors. They followed a humble path, seeking to be faithful in little things. They received a fantastic prophetic calling, yet they didn't use fantastic methods to achieve it. They humbly and bravely lived what they believed, passing on their beliefs to their success.

Our Founding Fathers took the Puritan beliefs, principles, and prophetic guidelines, organizing them into a secular government based upon those principles. They participated in all the institutions of our society and used them to guide and educate their countrymen on the new kind of government and the new kind of society. They didn't avoid intellectual controversy. They were not only spiritual but also the best and brightest of their generation. They were the influencers, the movers and shakers. So too, we need to impact the marketplace, news media, courts, education, government, and the arts and entertainment institutions with men and women anointed by God for their vocations in the secular world. Our ancestors cry out to us to keep religion and morality alive in our institutions. They expect modern believers to keep Judeo-Christian principles dominant in American culture and politics.

American Puritans transformed the world by following God's instructions to revolutionize the institutions of church and state. They were brave warriors who knew they possessed the calling to fight antichrists and antichrist systems. They are an inspiration for American Christians, who are also in a war with internal and external antichrists—socialists and secular progressives and radical Muslim terrorists. The next chapter presents inspirational information about the spiritual calling of Columbus, the Puritans, and America. The purpose of that chapter is to motivate the reader to follow in the footsteps of our Puritan ancestors by continuing to pursue God's prophecies and instructions for our nation as first proclaimed to those dedicated warrior-servants. Our national calling cries out for action. We are the remnant appointed to win the Culture War.

CHAPTER TWO

America's Prophetic Calling

God uses the events of history to accomplish His purposes. He inspires and proclaims His mind to His servants, asking for their cooperative obedience. Both Columbus and the Puritans obeyed God's calling on their lives. They received prophecies encouraging and guiding them. These prophecies came true, which is a sign of the validity of those prophetic declarations. Because of cultural and spiritual limitations, they could not envision how God would actually use those "islands" He sent them to discover and inhabit, but it didn't matter. They felt the same passion as Moses standing before the burning bush. They never understood the full implications of their actions because, as it says in Hebrews 11:13 about men and women of faith, "These all died in faith, not having received the promises, but having seen them afar off were assured of them, embraced *them* and confessed that they were strangers and pilgrims on the earth."

Columbus and the Puritans, not having full knowledge of how God would use America to astound the world, but having a clear vision of their being called by God, struck out for unknown lands to prepare a nation for God's use. The following dramatizations, first Columbus and then the Puritans, will hopefully transport you into their spiritual struggles and into their hunger to serve their Lord and King. Put yourself in their place and imagine the emotion behind God's prophetic messages. We have to also remember that these prophecies continue to hold true and continue to guide us as to how God wants to use America. Prophecies don't lose their validity and weight with time. They continue to demand accountability from their recipients throughout the ages; America continues to be called to fulfill the following prophecies:

God Sent Columbus

Slumped over the table, his head bent and shoulders heaving, Columbus struggles in agony, crying out to God, "Lord, why do you allow me to continue being laughed at and ridiculed? Is there no end to the mockery? The burning ambition you have placed in my belly will not let me stop making a fool of myself."[1] He scans the worn and ragged maps one more time. As he hammers the maps and the table, a look of weariness and frustration flickers across his face as he again pleads, "How much longer must I wait? The Holy Spirit illuminated his holy and sacred Scriptures with a very strong and clear voice, but it has been seven years without a glimpse of success."[2]

Christopher puts away his maps and begins to think about all that the Lord had shown him. He thinks back to the years of constant reading and studying "cosmography, histories, chronicles, philosophy, and other disciplines."[3] He movingly recalls how the "hand of Our Lord opened my mind to the possibility of sailing to the Indies and gave me the will to attempt the voyage."[4] Replacing the maps with his well-worn Bible, he turns to the thinning, torn pages of Isaiah. He has told Ferdinand and Isabella "that for the voyage to the Indies neither intelligence nor mathematics nor world maps were of any use to me; it was the fulfillment of Isaiah's prophecy."[5] Still, they continue to resist his plan to sail west to the Indies, even after he clearly and passionately revealed God's commission to reach out to the "islands."

He could not get Isaiah's prophecies out of his mind: Isaiah 42, 49, 66, and on and on. Christopher knew God gave him no choice but to seek the "islands." Even his name *Columbus*—meaning "Christ-Bearer"—spoke to him of his calling. The "islands" awaited his discovery so the Gentiles in faraway lands could be saved. To Columbus, Isaiah was not just a prophet but also an evangelist used by God to promise salvation to the Gentiles. He paces his flat with ferocity, waiting to fulfill his destiny.

Prophecy Understood

The dramatization above introduces the reader to Columbus's passion and motives. I took some liberty in expressing what I perceived Columbus felt, based upon his passionate defense and explanations for his exploration in his *Book of Prophecies*. God spoke to him through the Scriptures and through the writings of holy, respected men. Because of what Columbus read he was convinced God had called him to discover the "islands" or "coastlands." He thought he was going to India, but God knew he was sending him to discover the North American continent. Historians in recent years have painted a picture of Columbus as a greedy, power-hungry explorer. When reading Columbus's writings, however, nothing was further from the truth in his initial motivation.

More is known about Columbus since his *Book of Prophecies* was published in English in 1997. He revealed two main spiritual motives. Columbus followed a tradition of Middle Age prophecy that described certain requirements for the return of Christ. Columbus stated that God called him to provide by the riches from his discoveries the financial means for Spain to build an army to free Jerusalem from the Muslims. His other purpose was to evangelize Gentiles living beyond the present known world: "His is the beginning of the book or collections of auctoritates, sayings, opinions, and prophecies concerning the need to recover the holy city and

Mount Zion, and the discovery and conversion of the islands of the Indies and of all peoples and nations, for Ferdinand and Isabella, our Spanish rulers."[6]

Kevin Miller in his article "Why Did Columbus Sail?" further explains Columbus's motivations: ". . . we know beyond a doubt that Columbus sailed, in part, to fulfill a religious quest. Columbus's voyages were intense religious missions. He saw them as a fulfillment of a divine plan for his life—and for the soon-coming end of the world. As he put it in 1500, "God made me the messenger of the new heaven and the new earth of which he spoke in the Apocalypse of St. John [Rev. 21:1] after having spoken of it through the mouth of Isaiah; and he showed me the spot where to find it."[7]

Miller quoted Las Casas, one of Columbus's companions in his discovery and later an advocate for the Indians: "Columbus showed the way to the discovery of immense territories and many peoples are now ready and prepared to be brought to the knowledge of their Creator and the faith."[8] "As a sign of that work, on every island he explored, Columbus erected a large wooden cross."[9]

Before Columbus arrived back to the Spanish court at the end of his first discovery, he wrote a letter proceeding him stating, "Our Redeemer has given this triumph . . . for all of this Christendom should feel joyful and make great celebrations and give solemn thanks to the Holy Trinity . . . for the great exaltation which it will have in the salvation of so many peoples to our holy faith and, secondly, for the material benefits which will bring refreshment and profit."[10]

From the above, we can conclude that according to Columbus, God sent him to discover the New World. Why is that important? It's important because it helps define America's place and role in God's historical plan, which will finally result in the Lord's return. God has used nations for His purposes. Some He uses without their consent and others with consent and a covenant of commitment. Israel was the first nation called to be a covenant people with God, and the first nation God used with their consent. America is the other nation in which God entered into a covenant with a special calling for them to fulfill. America could be called the Gentile version of Israel, although with some limitations. For example, they didn't provide the line of descendants for Christ to be born. Later in this book, you will see the same Scriptures that Columbus received reappearing, as God speaks to the Puritans about His mission for them. These Scriptures involve the New World being a new heaven and new earth and also a missionary field for saving Gentiles. When reviewing God's plan for spreading the gospel throughout the world, Columbus could be seen as the "advance man for a mighty evangelistic campaign."[11]

Before moving on to investigate the role of the Puritans in God's historical strategy, we need to understand how Christians in the time of Columbus and the Puritans viewed post-Old Testament prophesy. It's similar to Christians today, but we use different terminology. Reviewing the teaching on *logos* and *rhema* helps validate Columbus and the Puritans' practice. In the New Testament, two Greek words are used for the term "word"—*logos* and *rhema*. Bill Gothard in his online essay "Understanding Rhema" explains as follows: "Those who hear the Gospel receive a special message from the Holy Spirit, for no man can call Jesus Lord, but by the Holy Spirit. 'No man can say that Jesus is the Lord, but by the Holy Ghost' (1 Cor. 12:3 KJV)."[12] Therefore, it's appropriate for the message of salvation to be *rhema*, or a personally applied word of God to an individual. Gothard continues to explain, "The word [*rhema*] is nigh thee, even in thy mouth, and in thy heart: that is, the word [*rhema*] of faith, which we preach; That if thou shalt confess with thy mouth the Lord Jesus, and shalt believe in thine heart that God hath raised him from the dead, thou shalt be saved. . . . So then faith cometh by hearing, and hearing by the word [*rhema*] of God" (Rom. 10:8, 9, 17 KJV; see also Acts 5:20).[13]

The *rhema* is God's word mixed with faith that causes a response from the hearer. It can be identified with the "word of knowledge" and "prophecy" found in 1 Corinthians 12. In the case of Columbus, he received personal words from God, applying certain Old Testament Scriptures to the founding and purpose of the North American continent. Most believers have experienced God's personal word to them when they are in a trial or seeking guidance: The Holy Spirit causes a Scripture or biblical story to come to mind or jump out at them while reading the Bible or hearing a sermon that addresses and answers their prayer request. New Testament prophecy as described by Paul in his letter to the Corinthians also depends upon *rhema*. Often in a prayer setting or congregational environment, the Lord speaks through prophecy to those present by using a reference to some passage of Scripture that had universal meaning when written or spoken but now is applied to a particular situation or congregation. These prophecies are a valid and true representation of God's will or plan, but they are not His *logos*—the total written word of God as applied universally.

Now, how does *rhema* apply to America's calling and relationship with God? It's important for Christians to know about God's calling for our nation as we see the Middle East heating up and potential signs of Jesus' imminent return. Has God called America to play a significant role in His return? Does the "a city upon a hill" image reflect a permanent and instrumental calling in God's end-times plan? Are there any scriptural references that can clarify and confirm our calling? These questions are important, since knowing our destiny will help us fulfill it. Otherwise we could yield to the secularization of our nation and lose our worldwide mission. What if in the future we turn against Israel or fall into complete back-sliding from our Christian roots? Will God forsake us and let us be crushed by the dark forces fighting against His Kingdom? Will our nation yield to the Antichrist and become God's enemy? I personally believe God has made a covenant with us and set His anointing upon us. American Christians have a responsibility to restore America to its Judeo-Christian principles, and to fulfill His covenant by fulfilling the specific instructions He initially gave to the Puritans. Now, let us move on in our search for our God-given mission by examining the Puritans' contribution to establishing it.

The Puritans Were Sent

Edward Johnson came to America from England with the first Puritans on the *Arabella* in 1630. Most historians are frustrated with his history because of some chronological differences with other histories. What these historians failed to understand was that Johnson's main goal was to present the prophetic and ordained nature of the Puritans' mission rather than a strict history, similar to how the Gospels were written to present the life of Christ in the context of a greater message to refute heresy developing at the time. He was not trying to write an accurate history as much as he was trying to reveal God's hand in the founding of New England and the special calling of the Puritans in coming to the island wilderness they came to call home (see Edward Johnson's *Wonder-Working Providence*). Starting with the title until the end of the book, Johnson describes in glorious terms God's wonder-working power.

In his history of New England, Johnson quoted original prophecies proclaimed by members in various meetings in England before they left. These prophecies instructed the Puritans on God's will for them and for their new community. I will use these prophecies and their interpretation to recreate the setting in England at the time they were given. The following quotation from Johnson's book sets the stage for the drama: "And therefore in the yeere 1628, he stirres up his servants as the Heralds of a King to make this proclamation for Voluntiers, . . ."[14]

Dramatization

A small group of believers crammed into the parlor owned by one of their members. It was growing late and the weariness of those present weighed upon them as they prayed. They felt wearied as well by the constant arguments and pressures from ministerial leaders in the Church of England to make them conform to unscriptural beliefs and rituals. Since the church and state were one, some believers had been jailed and others were living in fear. What were they to do? How could they escape persecution? Then, the Spirit began to lift the heaviness weighing down upon the seekers. One of their members who often received messages from God began to speak. He proclaimed with a strong anointing,

> Oh yes! oh yes! oh yes! All you the people of Christ that are here Oppressed, Imprisoned and scurrilously derided, gather yourselves together, . . . and more especially for planting the

united Collonies of new England; Where you are to attend the service of the King of Kings, on the divulging of this Procla-mation (prophecy) by his Herralds (prophets) at Armse.[15]

The members looked at each other with wonder. What was God telling them? Was he telling them to leave England, their cherished home? Was the King of Kings calling them to New England? How astonishing! Still, they trusted the messenger; he often spoke proph-ecies that proved to be true. What else did God want to tell them?

How much more shall Christ who createth all power, call over this 900 league Ocean at his pleasure, such instruments as he thinks meete to make use of in this place, from whence you are now to depart, but further that you may not delay the Voy-age intended, for your full satisfaction, know this is the place where the Lord will create a new Heaven, and a new Earth in, new Churches, and a new Common-wealth together; . . ."

"Search out the mind of God both in planting and con-tinuing Church and civill Government, but be sure they be distinct, yet agreeing and helping the one to the other; Let the matter and forme of your Churches be such as were in the Primitive Times (before Antichrists Kingdome prevailed).[16]

The congregation was stunned. How could God create a "new Heaven and a new Earth" with such a small, modest group of Eng-lishmen? Yet, leaving England could be the answer. They could fashion new churches and a new civil government. For years now they had been trying to cleanse out all Roman Catholic influences from the Church of England. By following the pattern of the earliest churches in Acts, they could complete and perfect the Reformation. They could also introduce England and other nations to the model for God's millennial government by forming a new kind of govern-ment in the New World. What an astounding idea! Tell us more, Lord!

And all you, who are or shall be shipped for this worke, thinke it not enough that you injoy the truth, but you must hate every false way and know you are called to be faithful Souldiers of

Christ, not onely to assist in building up his Churches, but also in pulling downe the Kingdome of Anti-Christ, . . .[17]

Everyone rose to their feet as one, raising their voices in praise. One member cried out, "We are your soldiers! We are ready to fight the Antichrist, O Lord! Send us! We rejoice in your calling!" All those present cried out with great joy and fervor, worshipping the Lord with one mind and voice.

They all began discussing with each other what they thought the prophecy meant. Should they be ready to take weapons with them to fight the army of the Antichrist? What did God mean? What did it all mean?

Then as calm came to the congregation, they sensed the Lord had more to say. They became quiet and awaited more instructions.

. . . his (Christ's) powerful Presence and Glorious brightnesse of his Gospell both to Jew and Gentile, shall not onely spiritually cause the Churches of Christ to grow beyond number, but also the whole civill Government of people upon Earth shall become his . . .[18]

and further:

Christ Jesus intending to manifest his Kingly Office toward his Churches more fully than ever yet the sons of men saw, even to the uniting of Jew and Gentile Churches in one Faith . . .[19]

Another member under God's anointing responded for the rest: "Lord, we are ready to reveal your glorious power. Use us to unite the Jews with your Church to prepare your Bride for your return. Use us to reach out to your ancient people, Israel. Let us spark their return to the vine by prospering us in this 'New England Israel.'

Although their bones shivered from the cold and their bodies weakened as the night turned into morning, these dedicated Puritans refused to stop listening until God had given them all his instructions. Their spirits were charged with energy, and they hungered to hear their Bridegroom speak.

37

Let your Profession outstrip your Confession, for seeing you are to be set as lights upon a Hill more obvious than the highest Mountaine in the World, keepe close to Christ that you may shine full of his glory, who imployes you, and grub not continually in the Earth, like blind Moles, but by your amiable Conversation seeke the winning of many to your Masters service.[20]

Overcome with the scope of their responsibility, the congregation fell quiet as they absorbed the message. They knew the Scripture to which the prophecy referred: "You are the light of the world. A city that is set on a hill cannot be hidden" (Matt. 5:14). Now they felt the depth of God's expectations for them to be a model and example for the Jews and the rest of the world. A voice in the meeting rang out, "We stand ready, Oh Lord, to remove ourselves to your holy wilderness in covenant with you, committed to become those lights upon the highest mountain in the world. We will be that 'City,' shining forth for the world to emulate and as an inspiration for many to be saved. We will be your faithful, holy servants—not grubbing in the earth—but standing tall in your righteousness in churches and civil governments, in community and service, and in winning souls to your kingdom. Amen."

We are not dependent upon Johnson's record alone to substantiate that the Puritans who came to America received guidance through prophecies. John Winthrop, the first and most admired governor of Massachusetts, also confirmed the fact that prophecies were given to the Puritans before they made the voyage to the Western world. In his book *The Puritan Origin of the American Self*, Sacvan Bercovitch documented Winthrop's statement:

" . . . Foxe pronounced England the elect nation, and the New England settlers, as we have seen, discovered in their migration, God's call to His redeemed, and the world-redeeming, remnant. Our undertaking, wrote Winthrop in 1629, 'Is to be a worke of God. . . . He hath some great worke in hand which he hath revealed to his prophets among us.' "[21]

Christians in the sixteenth and seventeenth centuries were no different from Christians today. We still have meetings between

Sunday services, and God still speaks to us through study guides and discussions, through the Scriptures, and through words of knowledge and prophecy as described by Paul in 1 Corinthians 12. There are times in history God uses a small group of people to do a mighty work. The Puritans who came to America were handpicked to put words and descriptions as well as actions to God's plan for our nation. The prophecy above defines five goals not only for the Puritans but also for America to fulfill. These God-ordained goals reinforce the belief in God's calling on America to be an instrumental player in His historical strategy.

Five Puritan Goals in Coming to America

The following explanation is based upon the prophecies above. With each goal, I have included the responsibilities that rest upon the shoulders of present-day American believers. God's purpose for America has not changed. The covenant lives on, and it's up to us to continue to fulfill America's role in God's plan. Later chapters will explain how we can fulfill our responsibilities.

I. They wanted to please Christ by cleansing their churches from practices offensive to Him. They felt the Protestant Reformation was incomplete because the Church of England retained some Roman Catholic rituals and hierarchical structure as well as being a state-supported church. The state and church were intermingled, causing secular and corrupting influences in the churches. The Puritans believed that the completion and perfecting of the Reformation was a requirement for the initiation of the millennium. God instructed them to make their individual lives—as well as the churches—holy and without blemish. It was a high calling to purity and holiness that could only be achieved through cleansing out what they saw as false Roman Catholic practices and doctrines as well as personal sin.

In addition, the Puritans related America's calling as a completion to the Reformation, by following Paul's statement in Romans 11:25–27: "For I do not desire, brethren, that you should be ignorant of this mystery, lest you should be wise in your own opinion, that blindness in part [of the Jews] has happened to Israel until the fullness of the Gentiles has come in. And so all Israel will be saved, as it is written:

> 'The Deliverer will come out of Zion,
> And He will turn away ungodliness from Jacob;
> For this is My covenant with them,
> When I take away their sins.'"

The Puritans believed it was their calling to achieve the "fullness of the Gentiles" as part of their role of perfecting the Reformation. Their idea of fullness didn't refer only to the number of Gentiles who would be saved, but even more so it referred to the heart transformation and purity of the Gentiles who are saved. They believed the new nation and its churches would fulfill those requirements by returning to the form of the apostolic churches and through sincere effort following Christ in all behavior and intentions of their hearts.

Once the nation and churches accomplished this fullness, the Jews would convert to Christ and join with the Gentiles, becoming Christ's bride at the end of the age. One statement in the Puritan prophecy defined the relationship of America's calling to the final salvation of the Jews and the return of Christ:

> Finally, all you who are now sent forth by Christ your Jehovah to enter upon a Blessed Reformation, if ever you will have the honours to be provokers of his ancient People Israel (who are againe suddenly to be honoured by him in believing) kindle the fire of jealousy in their brests by your Holy, Heavenly and humble walking, have you not the most blessedest opertunity put into your hands that ever people had?[22]

In other words, the Puritans not only had a responsibility to restore complete purity and simplicity to the church, but also their act of completion would set the stage for the re-grafting of the Jews and the return of the Lord. One of the later goals will cover the other aspects of the new nation's responsibility to the Jews.

The churches in America did become those cleansed churches, completing the Reformation as close to God's will as is humanly possible. The Puritans laid a foundation of purity and salvation through faith not works as well as avoiding a state church. They returned to the model of the early church, simplifying their organization and practices to allow for a more intimate relationship with Christ. There were no priests, confessions, or rites to stand between the believers and Christ. Every church had its own ruling elders, and there was no denominational headquarters ruling over or controlling them. Each congregation made a covenant with God and each other, upholding a very high standard for salvation and holiness.

Although denominations later developed in our nation, there remain many opportunities for individual, nondenominational churches to spring up and for others to break away. This practice has its shortcomings, but it does allow believers to seek greater holiness and purity if they experience corruption in their denomination or local church. These Puritan traditions continue to reinforce and renew Christian fervor in our nation. That is why present-day America—although weakened by the Cultural Revolution and Culture War—continues to hold on to many of its Judeo-Christian beliefs while most people in Europe, including Great Britain, have become thoroughly secularized.

Being aware of America in God's historical strategy should inspire American Christians to even more fervently desire holiness in our churches and in our hearts. In America, each generation of believers has the responsibility to continue to live in the footsteps of the Puritans. The covenant continues and the requirements are holiness, courage, and faith to live according to God's Word.

II. God directed the Puritans to seek out His will in creating a new kind of civil government. Our churches and nation entered into a covenant with God; it was a spiritual and federal covenant just as was Israel's. In other words, our nation was called for a special task, not just its churches. This covenant was no ordinary covenant. The Puritans interpreted it as being only a little less significant than the covenant God made with Israel through Moses. It was the Gentile version of Israel's covenant with God. John Winthrop, the first governor of Massachusetts, was their Moses. He was a man of lofty and most-respected character. In fact, the majority of the governors in seventeenth century America possessed exemplary character, setting the standard for how voters in the future should elect holy leaders. In fact, because of the holiness and sincerity of the first Puritans, they believed they were God's chosen Gentile people and nation— His New England Israel.

In New England, churches and governments had different roles but they complimented each other and worked together to promote God's kingdom and plan. What separated church and state was not a wall, but a bridge. There was never a wall of separation. The officials and policies of its government were to be inspired and molded by Judeo-Christian principles and traditions. That idea was at the root of the thinking of the Founding Fathers when they established our government. They depended not only upon checks and balances and separation of power for the success of our republican government but they also depended upon the goodness and holiness of its citizens and its elected officials.

The civil government developed in a similar manner as the churches. In each colony, church members elected a governor. The standard for holiness for the governor was as high as the standard for a pastor. Each colonial governor and council made decisions for the colonies, and most of the laws were biblically based. The colonists' goal was to create a form of government that would prefigure the kind of rule Christ would use after He returned. They also viewed the new government in the tradition of John Calvin. In his *Institutes of the Christian Religion*, Calvin declared about magistrates, "In a word, if they remember that they are the viceregents of God, it behoves them to watch with all care, diligences and industry, that they may in themselves exhibit a kind of image of the Divine Providence, guardianship, goodness, benevolence, and justice."[23] In other words, civil officials as well as civil government reflected God's image and heavenly government.

God's plan was to form a nation he could use to fulfill His historical strategy before His return. By the eighteenth century God's plan for America's form of ruling became clearer. He wanted to shape a nation in which religion could grow freely without government interference. It required fashioning a government without the rule of one or a few, but instead one in which the people ruled. Chapter three will expand on God's leading and involvement in the final constitutional government that became America's unique republic.

Because God's hand guided and influenced the development of our government, we have a responsibility to maintain the system developed by our Founding Fathers under God's guidance. We have a federal covenant with God, not just a spiritual one. We cannot allow secular progressives to undermine our unique republican system by turning to the courts to legislate away our rights or use legislatures to undermine parental rights and the institution of marriage. Since God has called our nation for special service, we have the responsibility to be knowledgeable and active citizens.

III. The prophecy above stated, "You must hate every false way and know you are called to be faithful Souldiers of Christ, not onely to assist in building up his Churches, but also in pulling downe the Kingdome of Antichrist, ..."[24] The fact that God ordained America to have a role in the battle against antichrists and the Anti-Christ has been forgotten throughout the centuries. It was difficult for the Puritans to understand what the prophecies meant since they were culturally and historically limited to the interpretations of their times, just as was Columbus.

It's very difficult to interpret prophecies with complete accuracy at the time they are given. The prophecies are accurate but the interpretation is always limited. The cultural and spiritual beliefs of the time restrict our understanding of God's intentions. The recipients of prophecies can only follow God's directions for the immediate time, not knowing their future consequences and God's bigger plan. So the Puritans fought the antichrists in the religious system they left behind, and they were ready to fight the Antichrist (for them the Pope), but their antichrists were nothing next to God's plan to use America to fight the antichrists in the twentieth and twenty-first centuries.

They could not see past their own worldview to envision God making a nation that would continue for hundreds of years without His return. They would never have guessed the plan God had for America. Our nation did end up fighting antichrists, but they were not the ones identified by the Puritans. History confirms that the aspect of the prophecy about the role of our nation to defeat antichrists was true even though it didn't happen as the Puritans envisioned. As we now know, His plan was to create a nation and government that would fight against antichrist systems of a much greater magnitude than the Puritans faced. America has saved the world from totalitarian dictatorships—the antichrist systems of Fascism and Communism—twice in the twentieth century. And presently it fights against the evils of radical, Islamic terrorists. God continues to use America to spread freedom and fight antichrists throughout the world.

We cannot allow any antichrist person or system impose itself on our nation or threaten our nation by imposing its system on parts of the world that will eventually consume us as well, such as allowing terrorists to roam freely throughout the world increasingly imposing radical Islam on nations everywhere. Like Soviet Communists, terrorists are tools of the devil, continuing to foolishly challenge God although they cannot win. However, God needs America as His instrument to fight against these antichrist systems and one day the actual Antichrist. God's covenant with Israel and America continues and must be fulfilled. Americans cannot allow themselves to be deceived and lose their resolve to fight the enemy.

IV. Many times in his book Edward Johnson pointed out that one of the Puritans' missions in coming to America was to unite Jews and Gentiles, referring to Paul's reference to the Jews being grafted back into the Vine once the Gentiles completed their fullness (Rom. 11:25–27). Johnson further confirmed this idea when he pleaded,

> And now you antient people of Israel look out of your Prison grates, and let these Armies of the Lord Christ Jesus provoke you to acknowledge he is certainly come, I [ay] and speedily he doth come to put life into your dry bones: here is a people not onely praying but fighting for you, that the great block may be removed out of the way, (which hath hindered hitherto) that they with you may enjoy that glorious resurrection-day, the glorious nuptials of the Lamb: when not only the

Bridegroom shall appear to his Churches both of Jews and Gentiles, (which are his spouse) in a more brighter aray then ever heretofore, . . .[25]

He is pleading with the Jews to be provoked and encouraged by these Gentile Christians in America to join with them to become the Lamb's glorious bride. Although large numbers of Jews or a remnant in Israel have not yet responded to that plea, still we see America has been Israel's strongest ally. This prophecy is continuously being fulfilled by the ongoing commitment America has made to the Jews and Israel. America is Israel's strongest and most faithful supporter and defender. It has been ordained to unite Jews and Gentiles through its support, provision, and example. America also provided a haven for Jews long before Israel received back its "promised land" in 1948. Jews and Gentiles are united through the American-Israeli relationship and, at some point in time, assuredly Jews and Gentiles will become of "one faith" as Paul prophesied in Romans. America's role is essential in leading the way and being an example for Jews and all Gentile Christians throughout the world to achieve the "fullness" required for Jews and Gentiles to share "one faith," preparing for the Lord's return.

The prophecy makes clear America's responsibility to the Jews. Other Scriptures also confirm that God's plan for Jesus' return includes the Jews and the Jewish nation. For example, the names of the twelve tribes are written on the "twelve gates" of Heaven, the New Jerusalem (Rev. 21:12). Americans must hold their representatives and administrations accountable to our commitment to Israel. We need not support their every action, but we should continue to help protect them from their enemies, who are motivated by the ultimate enemy of God.

V. The City upon a Hill image is normally quoted from the covenant written out by John Winthrop for the Puritans in 1630 and called "The Model of Christian Charity." However, the idea of the City upon a Hill was familiar to the Puritans as part of the prophecies they received before they left England, directing them to go to the New World. The following quotation is from "The Model of Christian Charity":

Now if the Lord shall please to hear us, and bring us in peace to the place we desire, then hath he ratified this Covenant and sealed our Commission, [and] will expect a strict performance of the Articles contained in it . . . when he shall make us a praise and glory, that men shall say of succeeding plantations: 'the lord make it like that of New England:' for we must Consider that we shall be as a City upon a Hill, the eyes of all people are upon us; . . .[26]

As mentioned above, Edward Johnson referred to the image of New England as a light upon a Hill. The City or light refers to the New Jerusalem spoken of in the New Testament and specifically in Hebrews 12:22 (NIV): "But you have come to Mount Zion, to the heavenly Jerusalem, the city of the living God." As mentioned above, the Puritans believed they were God's chosen people, similar to the calling of Israel—though not equal in covenant and calling to Israel. They had a divine election and "laid claim for themselves the identity of the figural Israel, where to be a believer was ipso facto to be a 'true Israelite,' . . ."[27] Therefore, the City upon a Hill—that is America—would prefigure the New Jerusalem or new heaven. By their example, many throughout the world would be saved.

Here Johnson summed up the whole picture including all aspects of the Puritan vision for the importance of their endeavor and what was expected of them. As we can see, the City image first laid a burden on America to prefigure God's plan for the final establishment of His Kingdom. In addition, it was not only about being a nation revealing God's goodness and glory, but also the nation would reveal God's judgment and justice when the country deviated from God's principles.

Our history is replete with examples of God's favor and judgment. Because of Christ's sacrifice and a consistent remnant of fervent Christians, America has not experienced the same degree of judgment for our sins as Israel did for theirs. Yet we can see in our history a revelation of God's character through His blessings and judgments. Early Puritans constantly sought God and held community meetings of repentance when they strayed from God and felt His judgment. They often interpreted God's character from an Old

Testament perspective. Through the centuries American Christians have become more balanced in understanding the merciful dimension introduced through Christ's sacrifice and have not experienced God's judgment as harshly as Israel. However, we have experienced His judgment.

The first and most devastating judgment occurred during the Civil War. More soldiers died in that war than any of our wars up to the present. Abraham Lincoln admitted we deserved God's judgment and that the same amount of blood might have to be shed by our soldiers as was shed through violence done to slaves for more than a hundred years.

Was the attack of 9/11 one of God's judgments? We can say that if it wasn't God's judgment, at least we know that God used it as a wakeup call. His wakeup call had an effect because we now see a shift in values by many young people. Since so many people lost family members in 9/11, family has become more valued and treasured. While the baby-boomers wanted to change the world, many of today's younger generation place the value of family first.

Of course it's difficult to know which of the storms, earthquakes, and other natural disasters have been part of God's judgment on America or used as a wakeup call. Throughout American history, our presidents and leaders have called for days of fasting and prayer when they felt God's just hand was disciplining us.

In spite of our shortcomings, the initial covenant of our Puritan ancestors lives on in our culture, and consequently we have been blessed more than any nation in the history of nations. We initially covenanted with God to love and serve Him and our neighbors, to love justice and to walk humbly with Him. That commitment has continued in the hearts of many Americans, even those who don't know the Lord. We still desire to be a good nation and people, and we give much aid to those suffering around the world. We have remained faithful to support Israel and to work to unite Jews and Gentiles. We also continue to send missionaries to convert millions every year and to send soldiers to fight antichrists in our war on Islamic terrorism. However, to remain true to our covenant with God and to enhance that City image, we have much to restore that has been destroyed by the Cultural Revolution, and if it grows stronger, we may turn God away from us. It's our responsibility to reverse the secularization caused by the Culture War. It's our responsibility to restore Judeo-Christian values to the institutions that influence American's values and beliefs, restoring those values to America's cultural foundation. American Christians have to come out of hiding and reenter the Culture War.

In the next chapter we will take a seat at the Constitutional Convention and relive the drama of God's intervention in a very human undertaking.

CHAPTER THREE

Constitutional Genius

A proper history of the United States would have much to recommend it: in some respects it would be singular, or unlike all others; it would develop the great plan of Providence . . . In my opinion, the historian, in the course of the work, is never to lose sight of that great plan. Remarkable interpositions of the Divine Providence are fine subjects.[1] (John Jay, delegate at the Constitutional Convention and later Chief Justice of the Supreme Court, written in 1809 in a letter to Rev. Dr. Morse)

B efore entering the Constitutional Convention, we need to understand in more detail how God uses history to fulfill His plan. He guides historical events to accomplish His purposes. Not only do the events establish His plan, but these events also prepare human consciousness to be able to understand and embrace His plan. The following is a very short explanation of how God has interacted with mankind through history.

Providential History

God writes history in the broad expanse of its events and characters. We discover God's plan for the future by interpreting and tracing what He has already accomplished in the past, using His biblical principles and insights to understand it. The most significant and peak events in history are very few when seen from God's perspective. They are God's *grand moments* in time.

Once Adam and Eve sinned, God's salvation plan, which is the guiding principle for history, began to unfold. The following is a short review of God's view of redemptive history: The first significant event of reconciliation was the covenant God made with Abraham and his descendants, resulting in the origin of the God-picked children of Israel. In addition, since Abraham's response to God was through faith, his descendants would include all, whether Jews or Gentiles, who would be saved by faith through a covenant of grace. God in His inestimable, unfathomable plan provided a salvation net flung over the sea of all humanity.

Covenant with Israel

The next God-significant event was the covenant He made with the children of Israel through Moses when He gave them the Ten Commandments, the covenant of the Law. Paul explained how part of the purpose of this covenant of the Law was to bring human beings to the awareness they could never obey the Law perfectly. God gave the Law to reveal to human consciousness that works could not attain righteousness. However, the Law and covenant also had another purpose for Israel. God used His relationship with Israel as an example of the covenant relationship He desired with humankind. When the children of Israel obeyed God, He blessed them; when they disobeyed Him, He punished them.

God used the Bible, or *Tanakh*, His prophets, and His interaction with Israel to reveal His will and character as well as how He would bless or curse those who broke the Law. In addition, and most important, He used those interactions to prepare Israel and the world for the coming of His Son—in human form—which was the next grand covenant event of human history. It took centuries of God interacting with humans and nations to prepare their conscious minds to comprehend His supernatural entrance into history.

The Son of God took on human form in order to fulfill the covenant of the Law so He could introduce the covenant of grace. All the victories, defeats, and discoveries of the civilizations that came and went before Jesus had meaning only in relation to how God used them to prepare for His Son's birth, death, and resurrection. After Jesus' death, resurrection, and the sending of His Holy Spirit to initiate the body of Christ, all future history took on meaning only in relation to God completing His plan of salvation through His Son and through His Son's return.

God's use of Rome is an example of God using nations and events to fulfill His plans. God prepared the Roman Empire to be a vehicle as He planned for the coming of Christ and the spreading of the Gospel. Jesus, and later the apostles, used the Roman roads and the stability of the broad Roman Empire to bring many to salvation. God prepared and handpicked the Roman Empire to be the conduit by which the salvation message could be spread throughout the Gentile world.

Protestant Reformation

As we proceed with our God-directed history, we find the rise and fall of the Christian message and body of Christ in the history of the Roman Catholic Church in the Middle Ages. During the medieval period, the body of Christ fell into rituals of works and heresies under the papacy, false doctrines of the sacraments, and a hierarchical religious institution. Of course, all church members were not lost during that period, but the preaching of the truth of the gospel was sparse. There were some saved within the church, but many were hindered from salvation by ungodly doctrines and practices.

Various reformers rose up from within to cleanse the Roman Catholic Church, but its hierarchy was too corrupt to respond.

Therefore, God called one man in Germany to challenge the false doctrines of the Roman Catholic Church. In 1517, Martin Luther came to understand current church corruption from previous reformers who questioned the false doctrines of the church. These reformers confirmed his personal doubt about Catholic doctrines and the papacy. This questioning led to Luther's nailing the 95 *Theses* on the door of the church at Wittenberg. This act initiated the birth of the Protestant Reformation—the next grand moment in God's historical plan. It was a renewing of God's covenant of grace through faith.

The Protestant Reformation caused a revolution and revival in the Western world. Through Protestant reformers, God reintroduced the world to justification, or salvation, through faith. The truth about faith restored the salvation message and offered spiritual freedom for believers. Christians no longer had to pay for indulgences, depend upon a priest, receive the Eucharist, or be baptized into the Catholic Church to be saved. According to a renewed and deeper understanding of Scriptures, believers were high priests and had the freedom to go to the Father through Jesus without requiring intercession from a priest, a saint, or the Virgin Mary. Personal access to God through faith was restored.

American Covenant

Despite the revolutionary and world-altering consequences of the Protestant Reformation, God was not yet satisfied with its results. He had another grand moment in mind that would complete and perfect the goals of the Reformation. The settling of New England (America) was the next grand moment in God's plan to complete the Protestant Reformation and prepare for Christ's return.

In the twentieth century, many students of American history focused their research America's founding on the goals and covenant of the Pilgrims. The Pilgrims mainly sought to avoid persecution and desired a place where they could have freedom of religious expression. They were very important, being the first to make a covenant and civil contract, but the Puritans had a greater impact on America's identity and calling. As we saw in the previous chapter, the Puritans were more educated and prophetically sensitive than the Pilgrims and contributed the fuller understanding of God's intentions for this new nation, although He established His covenant with America through both the Pilgrims and Puritans. His covenant with the Christians and nation of America was the last covenant-relationship God established with a nation.

Preparation for Writing the Constitution

"Search out the mind of God both in planting and continuing Church and civill Government, . . ."[2]

The Puritan prophecy above reveals the guideline imposed upon all future officials chosen to draft constitutions and laws forming civil governments in the colonies. For nearly two centuries, all colonists involved in forming America's civil governments in each colony were expected to search out the mind of God. In addition, as mentioned in the last chapter, civil government had to reflect God's image and heavenly plan for an earthly government. When the Founding Fathers arrived in Philadelphia in May of 1787, many of them may not have remembered or been aware of that prophecy, but God's purpose for a civil government had been ingrained into their hearts and minds through the faith and purpose of their Puritan ancestors.

Cotton Mather, in his *New-English History,* reminded colonists of America's unique covenant and calling in 1698, about the midpoint of the nearly two hundred years from the Puritans' prophecy to the Constitutional Convention. His history was very popular and reinforced the importance and special role of America in God's plan. It was a reminder that must have lingered in the Founding Fathers' consciousness, especially once they were at the Convention and concluded it was necessary to dissolve the Articles of Confederation and replace them with a new Constitution. Then they realized the significance and historic nature of their endeavor. In a letter to Benjamin Rush in 1811, John Adams reflected on the providential importance of the historical events in which he had been such an influential part, "I was borne along by the irresistible sense of the duty. God prospered our labors; and . . . I hope that the ultimate good of the world, of the human race, and of our beloved country, is intended and will be accomplished by it."[3]

According to Page Smith in his book *The Constitution,* the Founding Fathers did prosper the whole world through their labors. The U.S. Constitution combined the thinking of Plato, Aristotle, Reformation thought, John Locke, Montesquieu, and Newton's system of higher laws into an amalgam that resulted in a government with a balancing of powers. The checks and balances in the Constitution protected the rights guaranteed by God for the whole human race. Smith stood firmly with the Founding Fathers' belief they had been chosen for a unique moment in history. Their forefathers had laid the foundation upon which they were building a new kind of government, one for which the human race had been waiting.

The Declaration of Independence revealed and solidified eighteenth century colonial political thought. It placed the source of rights in God, not a king, not the people, nor the government. Rights were inalienable, or incontestable, because they were given by God to mankind. The Founding Fathers took that truth as a given and didn't emphasize or discuss it that much when outlining the Constitution. That is why they had to be reminded of a need for the Bill of Rights by Thomas Jefferson and James Madison when seeking the Constitution's adoption. They were more concerned with creating a government that would fulfill America's calling to the world and human race to extend freedom and equality while, at the same time, restricting the lawlessness of human nature. The goal was to create an orderly society without requiring rule by an aristocracy or monarchy. It required a new kind of government that guaranteed the rights of all citizens without leading to anarchy.

According to Page Smith, this government was the result of what he called a "Re-formed Consciousness." Historical events and ideas had re-formed the Founding Fathers' consciousness for that specific time in history, bringing together those individuals with their unique knowledge, spirituality, and genius. As Smith summarized:

These two streams—the political struggle against arbitrary power and the idea of higher or "natural" laws—having merged were amalgamated with the Protesting System or Reformed Consciousness, which took as a matter of course that ordinary individuals could form new communities and governments simply by agreeing to do so. And that these communities could at once claim all those laboriously accumulated rights of which we have spoken, confident that their ultimate guarantor was God himself.[4]

The Objective of the Constitutional Convention

James Madison sums up the problems facing the Convention and goals of the Convention in the Federalist Papers, number fifty-one, written as a defense of the Constitution after the Convention. It's a classic, often-quoted description of the dilemma facing the delegates:

> But what is government itself, but the greatest of all reflections on human nature? If men were angels, no government would be necessary. If angels were to govern men, neither external nor internal controls on government would be necessary. In framing a government which is to be administered by men over men, the great difficulty lies in this: you must first enable the government to control the governed; and in the next place oblige it to control itself. A dependence on the people is, no doubt, the primary control on the government; but experience has taught mankind the necessity of auxiliary precautions.[5]

Madison brilliantly expressed the goal and conflict of creating a republican government. Because of fallen human nature, one could not completely trust the people or those governing. The conclusion was that there must be internal checks and balances upon each. How to accomplish these checks and balances was the enormous and grand task put before the Founding Fathers.

The following dramatization will not include all the struggles and compromises in the Convention, but the one that caused the greatest impasse and nearly paralyzed the Convention into failure.

The goal is not to know everything about the Convention but rather, to grasp the Judeo-Christian influence on the Founding Fathers' perception of human nature, the hand of God in the proceedings, and the continued awareness of our nation's special calling from God. Let's enter the Convention and discover how they resolved their most controversial issue.

Dramatization

A small number of deputies straggled into Philadelphia on "Monday May 14th 1787, the day fixed" for the meeting of the Constitutional, or Federal, Convention. However, there failed to be enough states represented for a quorum. Finally, on May 25 they had a quorum of seven states and began the proceedings. Although they were slow to assemble, the task at hand brimmed with destiny. Their task promised moments of dissension and elation amid heated debates and a sweltering summer. John Adams, although unable to attend the Convention, enthusiastically summarized the feelings of the delegates:

> You and I, my dear friend, have been sent into life at a time when the greatest lawmakers of antiquity would have wished to live. How few of the human race have ever enjoyed an opportunity of making an election of government, more than of air, soil, or climate, for themselves or their children! When, before the present epocha, had three millions of people full power and a fair opportunity to form and establish the wisest and happiest government that human wisdom can contrive.[6]

Everything That Follows Is Drawn from James Madison's Notes of the Convention

On May 29, Mr. Randolph of Virginia, representing the Virginia contingency, steps forward to propose a drastic revision of the Articles of Confederation, one which would essentially replace it. His recommendation is motivated by the "difficulty of the crisis, and the necessity of preventing the fulfillment of the prophecies of the American downfall."[7] Shay's Rebellion and threats of secession make forming a new government a necessity. If they don't act, the union will be dissolved.

Mr. Randolph steps forward and humbly, yet bravely, presents the Virginia Plan. He enumerates the defects of the Articles of Confederation and then proceeds to present resolutions proposing and defining a new government. Out of fifteen resolutions, it only takes until Resolution Two to launch the point of opposition that divides the small and large states and threatens the success of the Convention: "Resolved the rights of suffrage in the National Legislature ought to be proportioned to the Quotas of contribution, or to the number of free inhabitants. . ." [8] Once Randolph reads Resolution Number Two giving voting power to the large states, the small state delegates become incensed. Pennsylvania and Massachusetts will always outvote and overpower them. This is unacceptable. According to Madison, "Here was the essential bone of contention that was to very nearly defeat the enterprise."[9]

After adjournment, during the night of May 29, the representatives from the small states passionately discuss the unfair representation, and on May 30 they press the issue about proportional representation. The Delaware delegates threaten secession from the Convention, leading Mr. Reed and then Mr. Madison to recommend postponement of this issue while they tackle more easily resolved recommendations. All agree and the Convention continues.

The Problem Returns

Although the postponement allows for two weeks of respectful and agreeable debate leading to great headway for many of the resolutions, still the representation problem lingers under the surface. On June 13, Mr. Paterson from New Jersey asks for an early adjournment so the small-state delegates can compose their plan in opposition to the Virginia Plan. He calls it the New Jersey Plan. On June 14, because of the intransigence of the large states, the small states present the New Jersey plan, which makes recommendations that will reverse most of the previous headway of the Convention.

Mr. Paterson says his plan "sustains the sovereignty of the respective States, that of Mr. Randolph destroys it: . ."[10] The New Jersey Plan proposes that "the articles of Confederation ought to be so revised, corrected & enlarged, as to render the federal Constitution adequate to the exigencies of the government, & the preservation of the Union."[11] In other words, leave the confederation in place and retain equal representation for all the states thereby, protecting the equal power of the small states with the large ones. An impasse continues that cannot be breached.

By June 18, nothing has been resolved, causing dissent and discord to increase. Mr. Hamilton adds to the squabble by disagreeing with both plans, but especially the one from New Jersey. He introduces his belief in a strong national government to temper the power of the states and of their corrupt representatives. He eloquently explains that these men have

> . . . the love of power. Men love power. The same remarks are applicable to this principle. The States have constantly shewn a disposition rather to regain the powers delegated by them than to part with more, or to give effect to what they are parted with. The ambition of their demagogues is known to hate the controul of the General Government. . . . All the passions then we see, of avarice, ambition, interest, which govern most individuals, and the public bodies, fall into the current of the states, and don't flow into the stream of the General Government.[12]

Doubt and distrust shake the commitment of the delegates. How can they reach agreement? The system being recommended to check the power of all the states, at the same time, strips the influence and power of the smaller states. "[Mr. Madison] begged [the advocates of the equal representation] to consider the situation in which they would remain in case their pertinacious adherence to an inadmissible plan, should prevent the adoption of any plan. The contemplation of such an event was painful. . ."[13]

Then the argument is made to the larger states for equal representation in the second house, the Senate. This would limit the power of the larger states and limit the power of the people to seek to redistribute wealth. On June 26, Madison passionately appeals to limit the self-indulgence of the masses as they grow in power and numbers. "How is this danger to be guarded against on republican principles? How is the danger in all cases of interested coalitions to oppress the minority to be guarded against? Among other means by the establishment of a body in the Government sufficiently respectable for its wisdom and virtue. . ."[14]

Plea for Divine Intervention

Tempers heat up and so does the convention meeting room at the end of the scorching month of June. On June 28, "At this stage, with the delegates deadlocked, Franklin makes his famous plea for divine intervention."[15] His plea reaches back to the prophetic reminder to: "*Search out the mind of God both in planting and continuing Church and civill Government. . .*"[16] Franklin also refers back to Winthrop's Modell of Christian Charity and the high calling of the constitutional delegates when he declares in the following speech that "our projects will be confounded, and we ourselves shall be become a reproach and a bye word down to future age. And what is worse, mankind may hereafter this unfortunate instance, despair of establishing Governments by Human Wisdom, and leave it to chance, war, and conquest."[17]

Dr. Franklin's speech is filled with wisdom and humility, differing from the overconfidence of his earlier years. Because it gives insight into the struggles at the Constitutional Convention, I have included most of the speech.

Mr. President

The small progress we have made after 4 or five weeks close attendance & continual reasonings with each other—our different sentiments on almost every question, several of the last producing as many noes as ays, is methinks a melancholy proof of the imperfection of the Human Understanding. . . . In this situation of this Assembly groping as it were in the dark to find political truth, and scarce able to distinguish it when to us, how has it happened, Sir, that we have not hitherto once thought of humbly applying to the Father of lights to illuminate our understandings? In the beginning of the contest with G. Britain, when we were sensible of danger we had daily prayer in this room for the Divine Protection.—Our prayers, Sir, were heard, and they were graciously answered. All of us who were engaged in the struggle must have observed frequent instances of a Superintending providence in our favor. To that kind providence we owe this happy opportunity of consulting in peace on the means of establishing our future national felicity. And have we now forgotten that powerful friend? or do we imagine that we no longer need His assistance.

I have lived, Sir, a long time and the longer I live, the more convincing proofs I see of this truth—*that God governs in the affairs of men*. And if a sparrow cannot fall to the ground without his notice, is it probable that an empire can rise without his aid? We have been assured, Sir, in the sacred writings that "except the Lord build they labor in vain that build it." I firmly believe this; and I also believe that without his concurring aid we shall succeed in this political building no better than the Builders of Babel: We shall be divided by our little partial local interests; our projects will be confounded, and we ourselves shall be become a reproach and a bye word down to future age. And what is worse, mankind may hereafter this unfortunate instance, despair of establishing Governments by Human Wisdom, and leave it to chance, war, and conquest.

I therefore beg leave to move—that henceforth prayers imploring the assistance of Heaven, and its blessings on our deliberations, be held in this Assembly every morning before we proceed to business, and that one or more of the Clergy of this City be requested to officiate in that service.[18]

A Godly Progression

A softer and more open spirit enters the Convention after Franklin reminds the delegates that "God governs in the affairs of men." The delegates commit to holding a special religious service on July 4 and from that day onward, the Convention was started with the reading of a prayer. On June 29, Mr. Ellsworth, making another effort at compromise, "moved that the rule of suffrage in the 2nd branch be the same with that established by the articles of confederation. . . . He hoped it would be the ground of compromise. . . . The proportional representation in the first branch was conformable to the national principle & would secure the large States against the small. An equality of voices was conformable to the federal principle and was necessary to secure the Small states against the large."[19]

On June 30, Mr. King observes "this to be the last opportunity of providing for its liberty & happiness: that he could not therefore but repeat his amazement that when a just Government founded on a fair representation of the people of America was within our reach, we should renounce the blessing, from an attachment to the ideal freedom & importance of the States."[20]

Distrust and dissension resurge to the surface as motives are questioned and human nature further maligned. Mr. Bedford from Delaware contends,

> If political Societies possess ambition, avarice and all the other passions which render them formidable to each other, ought we not to view them in this light here? Will not the same motives operate in America as elsewhere? If any gentleman doubt it let him look at the votes. Have they not been dictated by interest, by ambition? Are not the large states evidently seeking to aggrandize themselves at the expense of the small? . . . Interest had blinded their eyes.[21]

To prevent further dissensions, on July 2, Mr. Gerry from Massachusetts proposes forming a committee to reach a compromise because, "Something must be done, or we shall disappoint not only America, but the whole world."[22] The committee reports back on July 5, and even though some objections continue, the power of the protests weaken until a compromise is reached: The House of Representatives provides for the democratic representation of the people and provides power to the large states through proportional representation; the Senate allows for representation of the states

(protecting the power of the small states) with equal representation. Divine intervention and willingness to compromise saves the
work of the Convention and wisdom prevails. Relief, excitement,
and a sense of satisfaction uplift the delegates, who are now ready to
tackle less emotional and divisive issues.

Other questions were decided more agreeably through the rest
of July and August until September 8, when the Constitution was
turned over to a committee to arrange the style of the document. It
was completed by September 15, and awaiting final approval. A letter of transmittal of the work with its improvements was presented
for signing on September 17, 1787:

LETTER OF THE PRESIDENT OF THE FEDERAL CONVENTION, TO THE PRESIDENT OF CONGRESS, TRANSMITTING THE CONSTITUTION

In Convention
September 17, 1787
Sir,

We have now the honor to submit to the consideration of the
United States in Congress assembled, that Constitution which
has appeared to us the most advisable. . . .

In all our deliberations on this subject (rights of the states)
we kept steadily in our view, that which appears to us the
greatest interest of every true American, the consolidation of
our Union, in which is involved our prosperity, felicity, safety,
perhaps our national existence. This important consideration,
seriously and deeply impressed on our minds, led each state
in the Convention to be less rigid on points of inferior magnitude, than might have been otherwise expected; and thus the
Constitution, which we now present, is the result of a spirit of
amity, and of that mutual deference and concession which the
peculiarity of our political situation rendered indispensable.

That it will meet the full and entire approbation of every
state is not perhaps to be expected; but each will doubt-
less consider that had her interest been alone consulted, the

consequences might have been particularly disagreeable or injurious to others; that it is liable to as few exceptions as could reasonably have been expected, we hope and believe; that it may promote the lasting welfare of that country so dear to us all, and secure her freedom and happiness, is our most ardent wish.

With great respect, We have the honor to be, Sir, Your Excellency's most obedient and humble servants,

George Washington, President
By unanimous Order of the Convention.

His Excellency the President of Congress.[23]

Even after Washington's sensible and inspiring support for the Constitution, some of the delegates still resist signing the Constitution for various reasons. Dr. Franklin makes one last plea before the vote. He is too weak to read his speech, so James Wilson reads it for him:

Mr. President

I confess that there are several parts of this constitution which I do not at present approve, but I am not sure I shall never approve them: For having lived long, I have experienced many instances of being obliged by better information, or fuller consideration, to change opinions even on important subjects, which I once thought right, but found to be otherwise. It is therefore that the older I grow, the more apt I am to doubt my own judgment, and to pay more respect to the judgment of others. . . .

In these sentiments, Sir, I agree to this Constitution with all its faults, if they are such; because I think a general Government necessary for us, and there is no form of Government but what may be a blessing to the people if well administered, and believe farther that this is likely to be well administered for a course of years, and can only end in Despotism, as other forms have done before it, when the people shall become so corrupted as to need despotic Government, being incapable of any other. I doubt too whether any other Convention we can obtain, may be able to make a better Constitution. For when you assemble a number of men to have the advantage of their joint wisdom, you inevitably assemble with those men, all their prejudices, their passions, their errors of opinion, their local interests, and their selfish views. From such an assembly can a perfect production be expected? It therefore astonishes me, Sir, to find this system approaching so near to perfection as it does; and I think it will astonish our enemies, who are waiting with confidence to hear that our councils are confounded like those of the Builders of Babel; and that our States are on the point of separation, only to meet hereafter for the purpose of cutting one another's throats. Thus I consent, Sir, to this Constitution because I expect no better, and because I am not sure, that it is not the best.

... Much of the strength & efficiency of any Government in procuring and securing happiness to the people, depends, on opinion, on the general opinion of the goodness of the Government, as well as of the wisdom and integrity of its Governors. I hope therefore that for our own sakes as a part of the people, and for the sake of posterity, we shall act heartily and unanimously in recommending this Constitution (if approved by Congress & confirmed by the Conventions) wherever our influence may extend, and turn our future thoughts & endeavors to the means of having it well administered.

On the whole, Sir, I can not help expressing a wish that every member of the Convention who may still have objections to it, would with me, on this occasion doubt a little of his own infallibility, and to make manifest our unanimity, put his name to this instrument.[24]

After his letter is read, Franklin moves that the Constitution be signed by the Convention members. Three men don't sign the Constitution, but thirty-nine do, and history confirms which members fulfilled God's plan for this new kind of government that had begun with the Puritans and was now completed by men who may not all have been as dedicated Christians as those who originated and received the vision and prophecy. However, God always accomplishes His plans in all circumstances, and He even convinced Ben

Franklin, who was a deist, at least until his experience in the Revolutionary War and the Constitutional Convention. At that point he seemed to deviate from the deist belief that God doesn't involve himself in the affairs of men. God used him, other deists, and of course, many Christians at the Convention, to form a new kind of government modeled after His design.

Madison confirmed God's influence in Federalist Papers number thirty-seven: "It's impossible for the man of pious reflection not to perceive in [the ability of the delegates to reach agreement on the Constitution of the United States] a finger of that Almighty Hand, which has been so frequently and signally extended to our relief."[25] Our government has been a revolutionary force in the world that by its very existence pressures other governments to provide rights and freedoms for their people. It's a force, not of nature but of God, to extend a better life for all people on His earth until He returns.

The civil government God ordained in 1628 was completed. Because human nature leaned toward sin, it would not work perfectly, but as stated by Franklin, "I am not sure, that it is not the best." God got His government. The best it could be in a fallen world. He formed it to fulfill His purposes. He required our government and nation to become His instrument to accomplish future plans for greater freedom and prosperity for greater numbers of the common man throughout the world, to promote increased justice on the earth, to preserve and promote religious freedom, to support missions throughout the world, to fight against antichrist systems, to promote the union of the Jews and Gentiles, and to present a model for goodness and justice that would reveal God's character to the world.

The Constitutional Convention and the Constitution established a clear document that could became a model for the future of our nation and for the rest of the world. During the nineteenth century, Americans were forced to make a choice whether to follow the principles of the Constitution and end the tremendous injustice of slavery or dissolve the union. American's consciences and consciousness grew beyond their ability to ignore the principles of freedom and equality any longer. The majority decided for justice and continued to fulfill God's calling and covenant for our nation.

CHAPTER FOUR

America's Prophetic Calling Continues:
Nineteenth Century

In the last chapter, we reviewed how God used history to inform the consciousness of mankind and more especially that of the Jews and Christians. For example, the revelations of the Old Testament prepared human consciousness to receive and believe that the Son became man and died for our sins. Through God's interaction with Israel and by guiding history after Jesus' resurrection, we discovered how He prepared our Puritan ancestors to receive His post-Reformation instructions. All the ideas formed by God prepared the Puritans for receiving His prophetic instructions. They could not have received those ideas except He prepared their consciousness to receive them. However, as we noted before, even then, they could not understand the full meaning and future realization of those prophecies.

In other words, although God ultimately chose a form of government more in keeping with earlier models—Greek and Roman—they didn't evolve progressively into that era. God intervened in history to establish the form of government He chose to use for His purposes as and when He called Columbus, the Pilgrims/Puritans, and finally the Founding Fathers (England also laid much groundwork for the final American product).

Application of God's Prophecies in the Nineteenth Century

"And all you, who are or shall be shipped for this worke, thinke it not enough that you injoy the truth, but you must hate every false way and know you are called to be faithful Souldiers of Christ, not onely to assist in building up his Churches, but also in pulling downe the Kingdome of Anti-Christ, . . ."[1]

Let your Profession outstrip your Confession, for seeing you are to be set as lights upon a Hill more obvious than the highest Mountaine in the World, keepe close to Christ that you may shine full of his glory, who imployes you, and grub not continually in the Earth, like blind Moles, but by your amiable Conversation seeke the winning of many to your Masters service.[2]

Abolitionists

The 1800s provided many challenges for America. The nation was in its infant stage, and the government required testing and perfecting. Politically, the first part of the century compelled the Founding Fathers and the next generation to hammer out and refine how the government would work. It was not a pretty process, with anger and accusations appearing much like government today. However, their efforts led to other compromises that assured further health to our struggling republic.

Although events of great importance occurred during the nineteenth century, such as the empowering of the Supreme Court, expansion westward, a war with Mexico, a Second Great Awakening, and the Industrial Revolution, these events paled in importance when held up to God's model for this nation. He expected moral goodness to permeate the fabric of our society. We were called to be lights upon a hill. How could we be those lights and live in truth if we violated God's law of love? God's main goal during the first half of the 1800s was to prepare Americans' consciousness and consciences by removing any and all antichrist system from the fabric of our society.

In a short time after the writing of the Constitution, the defense of slavery wound its way into America's conscience, hardening it against the truth about slavery. Once the cotton gin was patented in 1794, the southern economy became increasingly dependent upon slave labor. As time passed, slave owners and numerous churches in the South looked for a justification for slavery—even using the Bible to condone it. Many traditional churches in the North and South didn't defend slavery, but, at the same time, didn't repudiate it. Slave owners' constant assertion that their actions were righteous and were supported biblically worked its way into many hearts and minds, dulling most Americans' sense of outrage for a terrible injustice.

The abolitionists emerged in the 1830s in response to the growing defense of this inhumane practice of slavery. Slavery was an antichrist system because the abusers stripped human beings of freedom and dignity and used Christ and the Scriptures as means to defend it. Many Southern slave owners practiced cruelty, injustice, and domination under the guise of godliness. In addition, as mentioned above, many denominations and Southern churches reinterpreted the Scriptures to sustain slavery. At the same time, the conscience of the American public, Christian or not, remained passive and weak. Consciences were hardened in fear of the conflict that would result from confronting the Southern states. Consequently, God inspired a small number of receptive Christians to awaken Americans' consciences. Protestors, called abolitionists, rose up as a voice "of one crying in the wilderness."

The most vocal abolitionists stood in the tradition of John the Baptist and the prophets of the Old Testament. They spoke God's heart to the nation to shake up and break down the human hearts hardened against His justice. He used honorable, principled, and passionate fanatics to get American's attention. They cried out for purity and perfection. It was their voices and message that broke through the hardness and cruelty that was violating our covenant and could have resulted in God's abandonment.

There were two strains of abolitionists: the anti-constitutional group under the forceful, charismatic leadership of William Lloyd Garrison, who sought to reach Americans through a solely God-based moral message. He believed in the Declaration of Independence with its God-ordained equality and inalienable rights. Everyone, not just white Americans, had God-given rights to freedom and equality. As time went on he became frustrated with the church and government in his "increasingly strident repudiation of all Christian churches and of organized government."[3] He and his followers believed in moral suasion without church support and political action. He used the pen, demonstrations, and speeches to carry his message. The first editorial Garrison wrote was for the first edition of the *Liberator*—an anti-slavery newspaper—that revealed his approach. He spoke in fervent, immovable, upright language:

> During my recent tour for the purpose of exciting the minds of the people by a series of discourses on the subject of slavery, every place that I visited gave fresh evidence of the fact, that a greater revolution in public sentiment was to be effected in the free states—and particularly in New-England—than at the south. I found contempt more bitter, opposition more active, detraction more relentless, prejudice more stubborn, and apathy more frozen, than among slave owners themselves. Of course, there were individual exceptions to the contrary. This state of things afflicted, but did not dishearten me. I determined, at every hazard, to lift up the standard of emancipation in the eyes of the nation, within sight of Bunker Hill and in the birth place of liberty. That standard is now unfurled; and long may it float, unhurt by the spoliations of time or the missiles

of a desperate foe—yea, till every chain be broken, and every bondman set free! Let southern oppressors tremble—let their secret abettors tremble—let their northern apologists tremble—let all the enemies of the persecuted blacks tremble. . . .

I am aware, that many object to the severity of my language; but is there not cause for severity? I will be as harsh as truth, and as uncompromising as justice. On this subject, I do not wish to think, or speak, or write, with moderation. No! no! Tell a man whose house is on fire, to give a moderate alarm; tell him to moderately rescue his wife from the hand of the ravisher; tell the mother to gradually extricate her babe from the fire into which it has fallen;—but urge me not to use moderation in a cause like the present. I am in earnest—I will not equivocate—I will not excuse—I will not retreat a single inch—AND I WILL BE HEARD. The apathy of the people is enough to make every statue leap from its pedestal, and to hasten the resurrection of the dead. . .[4]

Garrison was one of the men most instrumental in moving the abolitionist movement to later victory, but for this book, we will concentrate on the evangelical perfectionists who broadened the movement to the political arena. As a matter of fact, the abolitionist movement later split over the decision of some abolitionists to pursue ending slavery through political action. These evangelical abolitionists followed the tradition of the Puritan prophecies. They combined church and civil government to achieve their goals—desired to create a democratic government to prefigure the millennium. They returned to the primitive church idea—avoiding denominations as extolled in the post-Reformation Puritan prophecies—and were motivated by the calling for our country to be a model and light to the world. They were also fighting an antichrist system although they didn't use those words to describe it.

They went by many names: "comeouters," "the Abolition Church," and "perfectionists." They arose from the evangelical perfectionist tradition that taught the necessity and possibility of achieving holiness during this life. Part of achieving perfection required Christians to reform churches and government. When it came to government, ecclesiastical abolitionists bore the responsibility "to work within the governing structures, both civil and ecclesiastical. Christians were obligated to aid and to support human governments; voting was 'the highest moral power' that could be exercised, and it was the duty of each sanctified believer to vote righteously and to secure 'legislation that is in accordance with the law of God.'"[5]

Perfectionist abolitionists were pro-constitutional abolitionists who turned to the Constitution, and later to a political party to support their anti-slavery argument. These men and women withdrew from their denominations because their pastors would not preach an anti-slavery message. They framed their anti-slavery message in the language of perfectionism and holiness. They believed Christians should and could achieve perfection in this lifetime and one step toward perfection was to fight for the freedom and equal treatment of slaves.

They believed if a person were born-again, he had to be antislavery. Conversion projected a believer into resisting the immoral social institution of slavery. They went beyond a moral message to organize politically so as to use government to end slavery. Just as the Puritans believed in a civil aspect to their covenant and original prophecy, so also, these ecclesiastical abolitionists included political methods to obtain their goals. They formed the anti-slavery Liberty Party in 1840. Then in 1848 they expanded their platform by joining with other anti-slavery advocates who also championed other issues besides slavery to form the Free Soil Party that later joined with other opponents of slavery and pro-union forces to form the Republican Party.

These abolitionists were truly the John the Baptists of their time, just as Thomas Paine and Jefferson expressed that tradition to the Revolutionary generation. John the Baptist, the purist, uncompromising voice in the wilderness, prepared the way for Jesus. History reveals that God uses extremist and purist messengers to jar and prepare the public conscience before sending the voice of reason and moderation to facilitate the actual transformation. The Declaration of Independence preceded the Constitution, and the compromises and conciliations of Constitutional Convention made it possible to appropriate and accomplish the vision of the Declaration. So, in like manner, the abolitionists preceded the more moderate and "wise as a serpent" voice of Abraham Lincoln and the Republican Party, who accomplished the abolitionists' goal and God's vision.

In this chapter, I cannot re-create one actual abolitionist convention or meeting as I did with the Constitutional Convention. Therefore, I will take some liberties as I did with the Puritans, presenting a fictional abolitionist convention with the voices and expressions of many abolitionists who may have never been present at one convention at the same time. I will use writings as well as speeches of various abolitionists to launch the reader into the convention, as if present in those dramatic, spirited proceedings.

Those conventions were held in great numbers between 1830 and 1850. They were animated, spiritual, and emotional events, similar to Great Awakening camp meetings. They revealed God's early, radical messengers who were sent to prepare the way for the final blow to slavery. The end of the chapter will document less emotional and more moderate political messengers and instruments— the Republican Party and Abraham Lincoln—whom God used to finally untangle the evil threads of slavery from our nation's fabric.

Dramatization

Event: An abolitionist convention, organizing and motivating its participants to write, speak, and rally against all acts of slavery in their states and throughout the nation.

The date: sometime in the 1840s.

Where? Syracuse, New York, a center for abolitionist resistance.

Religious abolitionists from many parts of the country crammed into the convention hall, filled with anticipation that God's Spirit would be present to encourage and guide them for the battles ahead. They were God's soldiers and messengers, carrying His cross of freedom into the enemies' evil kingdom of slavery. Their goal: to condemn the evil of slavery in the South and to bring it down through moral and political combat.

The convention begins with Joel Tiffany, an anti-slavery lawyer. He is moved by his revulsion for the pain and suffering of slaves and his shame over America failing to be the Model for the world. He cries out to the people of America and demands the end of slavery:

> If the Constitution of the United States was formed for the purposes of establishing justice among its citizens—to provide for the common defense of its citizens—to promote their general welfare, to secure to them the blessings of liberty, and these guaranties were made for that end, then, most unquestionably, the Federal government have full power to secure these ends, through the proper departments thereof. . . .
>
> The only thing wanting for the protection of every individual in the full enjoyment of his natural and Constitutional rights, is a disposition, on the part of the people, to enforce the guaranties of the constitution. Let them no longer plead that they *would* do it if they could.
>
> They have the full power, but lack the disposition to exercise it.
>
> How long, we ask, have you, through Congress, had the power to put an end to slavery, and the infamous slave trade, in the District of Columbia? How long have you had the power to abolish the most disgraceful slave market of the world, in your National Capital? How long have you permitted that ten mile square, which, as the Capital of the "Model Republic," should have been consecrated to freedom, be desecrated by the tread of the infamous slave driver, and to drink up the life blood of the bleeding and crushed slave?
>
> How long have you serenaded your Presidents, Senators and Representatives in Congress with that music, whose treble, was the shriek of the slave mother, torn from her babe, whose tenor, the wailing of children forced from the affectionate embrace of their parents, whose bass was the deep, unutterable groan and anguish, of the heart-broken husband and father, as he surveyed the desolation of his household; and whose accompaniment, to complete the "Melody," was the cry of the Auctioneer, the falling of his hammer—the loud curse of the brutal driver, the clanking of the chain and

fetter, and the sharp crack of the bloody whip? We answer for *fifty years*!

For *fifty long years* have these scenes been daily enacted in your National Capital; before your eyes, and before the eyes of all the world, and *tremble*, faithless citizen, in the face of high Heaven!! For *fifty long years*, as an American citizen you have had the power to banish slavery, with its long catalogue of crimes, and woes, from that District; and yet you have refused to do it, lest you should trample the "rights, and immunities" of the bloody tyrant. For *fifty long years* have you been besought, by tears and groans, and prayers and heart-breaking agonies, to put an end to these things, by abolishing slavery in your National Capital; but you have turned away to fight a sub-treasury, or a bank, or to patch up a tariff. American citizen! Well may you "tremble when you reflect that *God is just* and that his *Justice cannot sleep forever. . . .*"

Be it known that, as American citizens, we have had the full power in our hands for years, to control, and put an end to all these evils, and nothing *but the lack of a disposition*, has prevented us from the exercise of that power—so that before God, and the world, the whole guilt of slavery rests upon our heads—the blood of six millions of slaves is now in our skirts; and nothing but the most bitter tears of repentance, producing, in us, the appropriate and necessary fruits, can remove that sinking burden from our souls. Else, like the ghost of Ann, to Richard, the boding cry of all these murdered slaves will come and say "let me sit heavy on thy soul" in Judgment.[6]

The clarity and conviction of Tiffany's words wound the hearts of those present. They fall on their faces in an act of repentance for the sins of the American people against those they have enslaved. The Spirit moves their hearts into deep crying and groaning. This anti-slavery body is not only a political body but also a church. They will not rest until they reform the American people and the government through their message of sanctification and holiness. There is no holiness without the end of slavery, and they believe the Declaration of Independence and Constitution support their goal.

They will use government to fulfill God's will to "set the captives free" in America.

As the spirit of repentance lifts off the anti-slavery congregation, the Spirit prepares them for His next messenger and message. Lysander Spooner, who looks to the law to support abolition, rises to cheers and excited expectations:

> THE practice of the government, under the constitution, has not altered the legal meaning of the instrument. It means now what it did before it was ratified, when it was first offered to the people for their adoption or rejection. One of the advantages of a written constitution is, that it enables the people to see what its character is before they adopt it; and another is, that it enables them to see after they have adopted it, whether the government adheres to it, or departs from it. Both these advantages, each of which is indispensable to liberty, would be entirely forfeited, if the legal meaning of a written constitution were one thing when the instrument was offered to the people for their adoption, and could then be made another thing by the government after the people had adopted it.
>
> It's of no consequence, therefore, what meaning the government has placed upon the instrument; but only what meaning they were *bound to place* upon it from the beginning. The only question, then, to be decided, is, what was the meaning of the constitution, *as a legal instrument*, when it was first drawn up, and presented to the people, and before it was adopted by them?
>
> To this question there certainly can be but one answer. There is not room for a doubt or an argument, on that point, in favor of slavery. The instrument itself is palpably a free one throughout, in its language, its principles, and all its provisions. As a legal instrument, there is no trace of slavery in it. It not only does not sanction slavery, but it does not even recognize its existence. More than this, it is palpably and wholly incompatible with slavery. It is also the supreme law of the land, in contempt of any State constitution or law that should attempt to establish slavery.
>
> Such was the character of the constitution when it was offered to the people, and before it was adopted. And if such was its character then, such is its character still. It cannot have been

changed by all the errors and perversions, intentional or unin-
tentional, of which the government may have since been guilty.[7]

Spooner's argument pleases the minds of those present. They
are convinced the Constitution supports their cause. John G. Fee,
another abolitionist lawyer, rises to defend the rights guaranteed by
the Declaration of Independence:

> Slavery is a usurpation of man's rights. That man, as man, has
> rights—rights variously termed natural, inalienable, inherent,
> or absolute—is a truth which has been conceded and acted
> upon by the mass of mankind, from creation's dawn to the
> present time. The law of God proclaims the same truth, when
> it declares, that God will be a "swift witness against those . . .
> that turn aside the stranger from his right." [Mal. 3:5] "To turn
> aside the right of a man before the face of the most High, ...
> the LORD approveth not" [Lam. 3:35, 36 KJV]. 'Woe unto them
> that decree unrighteous decrees, . . . to turn aside the needy
> from judgment, and to take away the right from the poor of
> my people." [Isa. 10:1, 2].
>
> In our Declaration of Independence, "the political faith of
> the nation," we have declared that "all men by nature are cre-
> ated equal, [that is, so far as are concerned, not as to condition;]
> that they are endowed by their Creator with certain inalien-
> able rights; that among these are life, *liberty*, and the pursuit
> of happiness.' These self-evident truths necessarily presuppose
> that man owns himself, for no man can have liberty without
> owning himself. . . .
>
> Again, the Word of God teaches that man as man owns
> himself when it forbids man-stealing. "He that stealeth a man,
> and selleth him, or if he be found in his hand, he shall surely
> be put to death." [Exod. 21:16 KJV] [Ed. Note: Also see Deu-
> teronomy 24:7].[8]

Someone cries out from the audience, "All people have inalienable
rights! We must win this battle against evil. God wills it! Yes! Yes!" A
chorus of voices rises, "God wills it! God wills it! God wills it!"

The abolitionists continue to chant while waiting for the next
speaker. Walking up to the platform is a small, young woman.

Everyone grows quiet as Angelina Grimke Weld takes the stage to begin her address. She and her sister are from families who owned slaves. They could no longer endure seeing their slaves in chains and so joined with Garrison to fight slavery. As she starts to speak, angry, pro-slavery men bang on the door and yell out threats at the anti-slavery delegates. Unmoved by the threats, she begins:

> Men, brethren and fathers—mothers, daughters and sisters, what came ye out for to see? A reed shaken with the wind? Is it curiosity merely, or a deep sympathy with the perishing slave, that has brought this large audience together? [A yell from the mob outside the building.] Those voices without ought to awaken and call out our warmest sympathies. Deluded beings! "they know not what they do."
>
> They know not that they are undermining their own rights and their own happiness, temporal and eternal. Do you ask, "what has the North to do with slavery?" Hear it—hear it. Those voices without tell us that the spirit of slavery is *here*, and has been roused to wrath by our abolition speeches and conventions: for surely liberty would not foam and tear herself with rage, because her friends are multiplied daily, and meetings are held in quick succession to set forth her virtues and extend her peaceful kingdom. This opposition shows that slavery has done its deadliest work in the hearts of our citizens. Do you ask, then, 'what has the North to do?' I answer, cast out first the spirit of slavery from your own hearts, and then lend your aid to convert the South. Each one present has a work to do, be his or her situation what it may, however limited their means, or insignificant their supposed influence. The great men of this country will not do this work; the church will never do it. A desire to please the world, to keep the favor of all parties and of all conditions, makes them dumb on this and every other unpopular subject. They have become worldly-wise, and therefore God, in his wisdom, employs them not to carry on his plans of reformation and salvation. He hath chosen the foolish things of the world to confound the wise, and the weak to overcome the mighty.
>
> As a Southerner I feel that it is my duty to stand up here to-night and bear testimony against slavery. I have seen it—I

have seen it. I know it has horrors that can never be described. I was brought up under its wing: I witnessed for many years its demoralizing influences, and its destructiveness to human happiness. . . . [Just then stones were thrown at the windows—a great noise without, and commotion within.] What is a mob? What would the breaking of every window be? What would the levelling of this Hall be? Any evidence that we are wrong, or that slavery is a good and wholesome institution? What if the mob should now burst in upon us, break up our meeting and commit violence upon our persons—would this be any thing compared with what the slaves endure? No, no: and we do not remember them "as bound with them," if we shrink in the time of peril, or feel unwilling to sacrifice ourselves, if need be, for their sake. [Great noise.] I thank the Lord that there is yet life left enough to feel the truth, even though it rages at it—that conscience is not so completely seared as to be unmoved by the truth of the living God.[9]

As Angelina finishes, quietness settles on the "congregation." Even the uproar from the outside is muffled by the presence of God's Spirit. Fear flees the convention as the Lord gives His messengers the feeling of peace and approval. They are wrapped in His pleasure and assured that their actions are righteous. Then slowly the glow of satisfaction is replaced by a new spirit, which rises up in the bellies of the participants. A spirit of repentance moves through the audience as God reminds them of Angelina's words—"This opposition shows that slavery has done its deadliest work in the hearts of our citizens." Many begin to groan as they beg forgiveness for those who have hardened their consciences to God's conviction. They cry out to God to save those who have seared their consciences and ask God to move them to repentance. They beg for the nation to live up to its vision that "all men are created equal" and possess "inalienable rights." They continue groaning and praying until their hearts are satisfied that God has heard them. By then the intruders have left and the convention continues.

Fredrick Douglass, a former slave, and warrior for abolition, slowly and magnificently rises from his seat to take the stage. He walks with dignity and with the air of someone who has been tried in the fire of affliction and been purified into gold. The convention-eers hold their breath in silent expectation of hearing from a man of great wisdom and knowledge, one who has lived as well as studied the moral truth about slavery. He begins:

> We, the people of these United States, in order to form a more perfect union, establish justice, ensure domestic tranquillity, provide for the common defense, promote the general welfare, and secure the blessings of liberty to ourselves and our poster-ity, do ordain and establish this constitution for the United States of America."

The preamble objects here set forth are six in number. "Union" is one, not slavery; union is named as one of the objects for which the constitution was framed, and it is one that is very excellent; it is quite incompatible with slavery. "Defence" is another; "welfare" is another; "tranquillity" is another; "justice" and "liberty" are the others.

Slavery is not among them; the objects are union, defence, welfare, tranquillity, justice, and liberty. Now, if the two last—to say nothing of the defence—if the two last purposes declared were reduced to practice, slavery would go reeling to its grave as if smitten with a bolt from heaven.

Let but the American people be true to their own consti-tution, true to the purposes set forth in that constitution, and we will have no need of a dissolution of the Union—we will have a dissolution of slavery all over that country.

But it has been said that negroes are not included in the benefits sought under this preamble declaration of purposes. Whatever slave-holders may say, I think it comes with ill grace from abolitionists to say the negroes in America are not included in this declaration of purposes.

The negroes are not included! Who says this? The consti-tution does not say they are not included, and how dare any other person, speaking for the constitution, say so?

The constitution says "We the people;" the language is "we the people;" not we the white people, not we the citizens, not we the privileged class, not we the high, not we the low, not we of English extraction, not we of French or of Scotch extraction, but "we the people;" not we the horses, sheep, and swine, and wheelbarrows, but we the human inhabitants; and unless you deny that negroes are people, they are included within the purposes of this government.

They were there, and if we the people are included, negroes are included; they have a right, in the name of the constitution of the United States, to demand their liberty. This, I undertake to say, is the conclusion of the whole matter—

- that the constitutionality of slavery can be made out only by discrediting the plain, common sense reading of the constitution itself;
- by discrediting and casting away as worthless the most beneficent rules of legal interpretation;
- by ruling the negro outside of these beneficent rules;
- by claiming everything for slavery;
- by denying everything for freedom;
- by assuming that the constitution does not mean what it says;
- and that it says what it does not mean;
- by disregarding the written constitution; and
- interpreting it in the light of a secret understanding.

It's by this *mean, contemptible, under-hand way of working out the pro-slavery character of the constitution, that the thing is accomplished, and in no other way.* The first utterance of the instrument itself [the preamble] is gloriously on the side of liberty, and diametrically opposed to the thing called slavery in the United States.[10]

The convention ends with a final burst of applause and enthusiastic appreciation for God's mighty messengers. Their mission was reinforced and their hearts encouraged. They left with the resolve to continue battling for their just cause. They knew God was with them in their righteous endeavor, and that nothing would stop them until they achieved victory. They were heartened and enlightened and ready to confront the nation with its sin and its failure to live up to its calling, to be the City upon a Hill and God's instrument to broaden the cause of freedom.

Republican Party and Abraham Lincoln

The anti-constitutional abolitionists, led by William Lloyd Garrison, remained a strong voice until the end of the Civil War. Garrison produced the anti-slavery magazine *The Liberator* and co-founded the American Anti-Slavery Society. He would not compromise his radical, righteous position against slavery and for women's rights. He and his followers were true heroes for freedom. However, it was the abolitionist church, or perfectionist abolitionists, that continued the prophetic tradition of combining church with government to remove moral imperfections from society.

The church in this case didn't mean traditional denominations, but it meant the Christians who left denominations and formed new churches and a political party to rally against slavery. Perfectionist Christians held up the moral standard and used government through politics to fulfill their goals. Just as God spoke to the Puritans that He had not only called churches in America but also the commonwealth of America to shine upon the hill, so also these anti-slavery perfectionists continued in that prophetic calling. They formed the Liberty Party in 1840 with its central message being abolition of slavery. Alvin Stewart, a writer and lawyer defined its goal when he wrote,

> The liberty party hold the Constitution of the United States to be, properly interpreted, an anti-slavery document, replete with tendencies in favor of freedom; but that the slaveholding portion of this country have seized upon the reins of government, and perverted the Constitution's high intent, to the base purposes of sustaining, and increasing the power of slaveholders in every possible way, and have violated the Constitution by employing it to sanction slavery in many ways, and in the overthrow of the right of petition."[11]

Because the Liberty Party didn't have much success in the 1840 and 1844 elections, they joined with other groups in society to form the Free Soil Party in 1848 and finally the Republican Party in 1854. The platform of these political parties was broader than the Liberty Party, but all of them were anti-slavery. The perfectionists succeeded in carrying their message to the nation in a valid and in the end successful political institution, the Republican Party.

Abraham Lincoln became the voice of the Republican Party. He tried, as did the Party, to present a message of reason that maintained moral goals but offered compromise as well. The political justification for the formation of the Republican Party was not the direct issue of ending slavery. Instead, the Kansas Nebraska Act became the point of contention and the magnate for anti-slavery forces. Lincoln declared he would not resist the Missouri Compromise that had for years retained but limited slavery. His argument stated that the Kansas Nebraska Act revealed the desperate and malevolent measure to which the South would stoop to spread the evil system of slavery.

The North suspected the South didn't want only the South and border states to be slave states, but that they wanted all states to allow slavery; in other words, the South wanted the nation to be a slave nation. As Lincoln expressed in his debate with Stephen Douglas in Peoria in 1854,

> This (the Kansas Nebraska Act) is the *repeal* of the Missouri Compromise. The foregoing history may not be precisely accurate in every particular; but I am sure it is sufficiently so, for all the uses I shall attempt to make of it, and in it, we have before us, the chief material enabling us to correctly judge whether the repeal of the Missouri Compromise is right or wrong. I think, and shall try to show, that it's wrong; wrong in its direct effect, letting slavery into Kansas and Nebraska— and wrong in its prospective principle, allowing it to spread to every other part of the wide world, where men can be found inclined to take it.[12]

Lincoln went on in this debate to express his own and the views of the Republican Party. The themes of America's founding are echoed throughout this debate. He was moved by the goal of America's prophetic calling as stated in the second chapter by Edward Johnson: "Let your Profession outstrip your Confession, for seeing you are to be set as lights upon a Hill more obvious than the highest Mountaine in the World, keepe close to Christ that you may shine full of his glory, who imployes you, and grub not continually in the Earth, like blind Moles, but by your amiable Conversation seeke the winning of many to your Masters service."[13]

Lincoln turned to this same theme when he pleaded: "Fellow countrymen—Americans south, as well as north, shall we make no effort to arrest this? Already the liberal party throughout the world express the apprehension 'that the one retrograde institution in America, is undermining the principles of progress, and fatally violating the noblest political system the world ever saw. . .' Our republican robe is soiled, and trailed in the dust. Let us repurify it. Let us turn and wash it white, in the spirit, if not the blood, of the Revolution. Let us turn slavery from its claims of 'moral right,' back upon its existing legal rights, and its arguments of necessity."[14]

And at an earlier time he declared:

"I hate it [slavery] because of the monstrous injustice of slavery itself. I hate it because it deprives our republican example of its just influence in the world—enables the enemies of free institutions, with plausibility, to taunt us as hypocrites."[15]

Although Lincoln tried to walk on the edge of declaring his intentions as president or the Republican Party's intentions to end slavery, he did express principles that, when followed to their logical conclusion, would require the abolition of slavery. Freedom had been an important value for the Puritans, seeing that they were seeking freedom to worship in their own manner. God expanded the idea of freedom through the seventeenth and eighteenth centuries, culminating in the Declaration of Independence. Increasing liberty became a moral issue and a moral right. Now the pressure was on the South to either restrain their demands for the expansion of slavery or suffer the consequences of their immorality. Once they identified slavery with definition of morality, they could not stop with limiting slavery to the territories of the Missouri Compromise. Since they had deceived themselves into believing that right was on their side, there was no reason to limit slavery at all. With their logic, eventually they had to press for slavery in every state in the United States. Lincoln discerned this progression when he said,

> I particularly object to the NEW position which the avowed principle of this Nebraska law gives to slavery in the body politic. I object to it because it assumes that there CAN be MORAL RIGHT in the enslaving of one man by another. I object to it as a dangerous dalliance for a few [free?] people—a sad evidence that, feeling prosperity we forget right—that liberty, as a principle, we have ceased to revere.[16]

Lincoln and the Republican Party for which he was a spokesman traveled on a path that had to lead to war not unity. The South knew the true significance of Lincoln's election as President. They were prepared to leave the Union once he was elected. They didn't wait to see what he and the Republicans were going to do. They knew already that union was impossible. They knew Lincoln's speeches and knew what his conscience would lead him to do. They remembered when he said in 1858, "Our reliance is in the love of liberty which God has planted in our bosoms. Our defense is in the preservation of the spirit which prizes liberty as the heritage of all men, in all lands, everywhere. Destroy this spirit, and you have planted the seeds of despotism around your own doors."[17]

They knew his hatred of slavery meant the end of slavery. Lincoln was formed by Puritan principles now so deeply embedded in the culture he probably didn't identify them. He could relate his beliefs to the Founding Fathers, but he was more than their product. He was formed in the bosom of God's prophetic vision for America. He was chosen to synthesize and moderate the abolitionists' demands. He was used to accomplish the death of the antichrist system of slavery and to reestablish America's position as the moral, shining city of righteousness and liberty. How do we know what his true feelings were about slavery? He was finally able to clearly express them in 1864: "I am naturally anti-slavery. If slavery is not wrong, nothing is wrong. I can not remember when I didn't so think, and feel."[18]

CHAPTER FIVE

America's Prophetic Calling Continues:
Twentieth and Twenty-First Centuries

"Little children, it is the last hour; and as you have heard that the Antichrist is coming, even now many antichrists have come, by which we know that it is the last hour" (1 John 2:18).

"This is how you can recognize the Spirit of God: Every spirit that acknowledges that Jesus Christ has come in the flesh is from God, but every spirit that does not acknowledge Jesus is not from God. This is the spirit of the antichrist, which you have heard is coming and even now is already in the world" *(1 John 4:2–3 NIV).*

"And all you, who are or shall be shipped for this worke, thinke it not enough that you injoy the truth, but you must hate every false way and know you are called to be faithful Souldiers of Christ, not onely to assist in building up his Churches, but also in pulling downe the Kingdome of Anti-Christ . . ."[1]

"An now you antient people of Israel look out of your Prison grates, let these Armies of the Lord Christ Jesus provoke you to acknowledge he is certainly come, and I and speedily he doth come to put life into your dry bones . . . when not only the Bride groom shall appear to his Churches both of *Jews and Gentiles.*"[2]

O f the five callings listed in chapter two, America had concentrated much of its energies on just three of them during the first few centuries of its existence. God had not called upon Americans to fight external antichrists or antichrist systems from the 1600s to 1800s. He had also not called upon Americans to protect or serve the Jewish people, except to provide a place of safety for Jewish immigrants. The twentieth century changed God's emphasis and increased the importance of these two callings. It was then that the United States was called to fight antichrists and save the Jews from total extinction.

Antichrists can be men or systems and sometimes both. According to John, the spirit of Antichrist denies that Jesus has come in the flesh. The spirit of Antichrist is different than an antichrist or an antichrist system. It prepares the way for the latter. It's not a demonic spirit or even Satan directly. It can be seen as a growing consciousness and acceptance of Satan's plan.

As mentioned earlier, God used the Jews and the Old Testament to enlarge human consciousness to grasp and accept the entrance of the Son into human form through a virgin's womb, His death on the cross, and His resurrection. These and other events were all prophesied in the Old Testament. Satan has his counterfeit plan and method of preparing the human race to accept the final Antichrist. Satan has used antichrists and antichrist systems throughout the centuries to prepare human consciousness to accept the Beast, or final Antichrist. It can be a New Age blend of prophetic or sage-like figures or an occult rendering of Christ as a false Messiah inhabiting some leader.

There are three examples of antichrist systems and two antichrists in the twentieth century. Nazism and Fascism were antichrist systems and Adolf Hitler and, to a lesser extent, Benito Mussolini, were antichrists. Communism stands as an example of a third antichrist system, and although Lenin and Stalin had antichrist qualities, they were not antichrists in the same manner as Hitler and Mussolini. The Soviet leaders were more servants of the pre-formed communist ideas as described by Marx and Engels while Hitler and Mussolini were instrumental in formulating, creating, and initiating their idolatrous systems.

In this book Mussolini's role will not be covered since it was secondary in power and importance to Hitler's. I will concentrate on analyzing the role of Hitler, Nazism, and communism in the rise of antichrists in the twentieth century and then explain America's role in fighting them.

The allied nations fought World War II not only to stop Hitler from expanding German rule around the world but also to stop his determination to exterminate the Jews. If Hitler had ruled the world, all Jews would have been exterminated. Therefore, in my opinion, God pulled America into World War II, not only to save large parts of the world from Germany and Japan's efforts to swallow up many nations, but even more so to save the Jews from extinction.

According to Puritan prophecy, America was not only a tool to fight against antichrists but also called to unite Jews and Gentiles. America the nation and its Christian servants were called to achieve the fullness of the Gentiles as described in Romans 11: 25–26 in preparation for the grafting back in of the Jews. Once the fullness of the Gentiles is complete, the Jews will be restored and renewed through a reconnection to the Vine. America's present involvement with and support of Israel expresses that ongoing mission. It's expressed in the union of the nation of America with the cause and protection of Israel as prophesied by the Puritans.

America's Role in Saving the Jews from Extermination

When America joined the Allies in World War II, our nation continued to fulfill its prophetic calling as one of God's instruments to fight against Satan's plan to exterminate God's chosen people. At the time, we didn't fully realize Hitler's plan to exterminate all Jews throughout the world. Therefore, we responded to the cry for help from Europe and Great Britain more than from the plight of the Jews. Only later was Hitler's evil plan of genocide exposed to the world.

Some historians and researchers think Hitler was influenced by the occult and gnosticism. We don't need any obscure writings or conversations about the occult to know Hitler's plan for the Jewish people throughout the countries Hitler invaded. He expressed his antagonism and prejudice toward the Jews in his book *Mein Kampf*. In it, he revealed his deep hatred, distrust, and disgust for Jews.

We must enter the mind of Hitler to truly understand Satan's plan for the Jews. First, I will give a summary of his thinking and then dramatize an interview with Hitler to convey the true evil of his vision.

Hitler believed that the Germans were related to the Aryans, connected to the Indian racial ideas of a pure race. The idea was that "pure, noble blood" would remove mankind from a corrupted world. A pure-blooded race that rules the world would free mankind from the material world and allow humanity to escape anti-spiritual elements that weighted down the human race and kept it from rising to its more perfect state. According to Hitler's thinking, the Jews were a major source for the corrupted blood of mankind and their God— Jehovah was actually Satan not God. Any intermarriage between Jew and Gentile caused a corruption of the blood for that family forever and interfered with mankind's escaping the captivity of the spirit in matter and the coming of an age of human perfection.

Throughout *Mein Kampf*, Hitler referred to the Zionists. During the 1930s, anti-Semites didn't believe that the goal of Zionists was to establish a state for Jews in Palestine. Many conspiracy theorists had felt greatly threatened by the Zionist movement. They claimed that the goal of Zionists was to take over the world through subterfuge. Hitler bought into these suspicions because of his own inferiority and desire to have a scapegoat.

An Interview with Hitler

The following fictional interview introduces the reader into Hitler's mind and the twisted thoughts that consumed it. His value and worth depended upon his view of his role in releasing the divine spirit of man from the material, evil world through the spread of Nazi spirituality and domination of the world by Germany. He identified himself as a promised messiah to save the world from the blood contamination of the Aryan race.

Questioner: Mein Führer, what do you see as the reason Germany lost to the Allies in the First World War?

Hitler: If we pass all the causes of the German collapse in review, the ultimate and most decisive remains the failure to recognize the racial problem and especially the Jewish menace.

The defeats on the battlefield in August 1918 would have been child's play to bear. They stood in no proportion to the victories of our people. It was not they that caused our downfall. No, it was brought about by that power which prepared these defeats by systematically over many decades robbing our people of the political and moral instincts and forces that alone make nations capable and hence worthy of existence.

In heedlessly ignoring the question of the preservation of the racial foundations of our nation, the old Reich disregarded the sole right that gives life in this world. Peoples which bastardize themselves, or let themselves be bastardized, sin against the will of eternal Providence, and when their ruin is encompassed by a stronger enemy it is not an injustice done to them, but only the restoration of justice. If a people no longer wants to respect the Nature-given qualities of its being that root in its blood, it has no further right to complain over the loss of its earthly existence.

The lost purity of the blood alone destroys inner happiness forever, plunges man into the abyss for all time, and the consequences can nevermore be eliminated from body and spirit.[3]

Questioner: Why is pure blood so important?

Hitler: All great cultures of the past perished only because the originally creative race died out from blood poisoning. All the human culture, all the results of art, science, and technology that we see before us today, are almost exclusively the creative product of the Aryan. This very fact admits of the not unfounded inference that he alone was the founder of all higher humanity, therefore representing the prototype of all we understand by the word 'man.' . . . Exclude him and perhaps after a few thousand years darkness will again descend on the earth, human culture will pass, and the world turn to a desert.[4]

Questioner: If the Aryan is the example of pure blood and superior to all others, why isn't the Aryan race dominating the world today?

Hitler: Often in a few millenniums or even centuries they create cultures which originally bear all the inner characteristics of their nature, adapted to the above-indicated special qualities of the soil and subjected beings. In the end, however, the conquerors transgress against the principle of blood purity, to which they had first adhered; they begin to mix with the subjugated inhabitants and thus end their own existence; for the fall of man in paradise has always been followed by expulsion.[5]

Questioner: Who is the greatest threat to retaining pure blood and to the preservation of the Aryan race?

Hitler answers with an example:

With satanic joy in his face, the black-haired Jewish youth lurks in wait for the unsuspecting girl whom he defiles with his blood, thus stealing her from her people. With every means he tries to destroy the racial foundations of the people he has set out to subjugate. Just as he himself systematically ruins women and girls, he does not shrink back from pulling down the blood barriers for others, even on a large scale. It was and it is Jews who bring the Negroes into the Rhineland, always with the same secret thought and clear aim of ruining the hated white race by the necessarily resulting bastardization, throwing it down from its cultural and political height, and himself rising to be its master.

Hitler continues:

For a racially pure people conscious of its blood can never be enslaved by the Jew. In this world he will forever be master over bastards and bastards alone. And so he tries systematically to lower the racial level by a continuous poisoning of individuals.[6]

Questioner: What do the Jews represent in nature and can they join the German people in their call to fulfill God's plan for a pure race?

Hitler: No! . . Two worlds face one another—the men of God and the men of Satan! The Jew is the anti-man, the creature of another god. He must have come from another root of the human race. I stood the Aryan and the Jew over against each other, and if I call one of them a human being I must call the other something else. The two are as widely separated as man and beast. Not that I would call the Jew a beast. He is much further from the beasts than we Aryans. He is a creature outside nature and alien to nature.[7]

From the above dramatization, it's clear what role the Western world and America played in God's plan. Hitler, an antichrist, was determined to cleanse the blood of Germans and Aryan races throughout the world by exterminating the Jews and other so-called inferior, non-Aryan races. As mentioned in the beginning of this book, America had a national and spiritual calling. The Puritan prophecy instructed our country to be tied to the fate and success of the Jewish people as well as fight against antichrists. In World War II, God used America to assure the defeat of the antichrists Mussolini and Hitler and to preserve the Jewish people throughout the world. In 1948, the United States was the first nation to recognize Israel as a state.

Further Fights against Antichrists

Once America defeated Hitler and the antichrist systems of Nazism and Fascism, it faced another antichrist system. After World War II America and Europe entered a new war—the Cold War against the Soviet Union and Communist China. The system of communism was an antichrist system whose goal was to impose totalitarian communism on states throughout the world. Its purposes were described more fully in chapter one.

The United States and to a lesser degree other European nations developed a strategy to defeat the Soviet plan without initiating nuclear war. For a little over forty years America fought the Cold War with victories and defeats. The policies of containment, the domino theory, and brinkmanship were not always accurate. Our leaders believed that if we didn't contain communism then once one nation fell in one territory, all would fall like dominoes. Then a whole continent would be under communist control. That was the theory behind saving Vietnam; we believed that once Vietnam fell all of the countries in Southeast Asia would fall under communist rule.

The theory was partially true. Yes, other nations in an area fell to communism when one began the trend, but it was not as extreme as we thought would happen. At the same time, if we had not supported states being threatened by communism, many more would have fallen and consequently, might have provided the support the Soviet Union needed to continue to survive and flourish. Containment and the domino theory didn't prove to be 100 percent necessary to stop communism, but overall, the plan worked through various circumstances and adjustments. Without those theories and actions taken to support them, communism may have continued to thrive into the twenty-first century.

Communism in Russia failed economically because a communist economic system could not work; however, America helped by challenging its economy and exposing its weaknesses. In hindsight one can see that God used the United States and Great Britain to promote and plan a method to defeat the antichrist system of communism. President Reagan and Margaret Thatcher (the prime minister in England in the 1980s), were instrumental, although not alone, in pounding the final nails to defeat Soviet Communism. However, as seen in the first chapter, some of the antichrist communist ideas continue to dominate our culture in certain areas.

A Further Call to Righteousness

The twentieth century also required our nation and its people to take another step "to live justly, to love mercy and to walk humbly with our God," as quoted in John Winthrop's *A Model of Christian Charity*. This quotation summarized the actions required for our nation to live up to its image of A City on a Hill. Living justly demanded that the mistreated and disenfranchised African Americans and other minorities in America be given full rights of citizenship. Slavery ended in the nineteenth century, but full rights and integration for blacks and other minorities had not yet been accomplished. Civil rights and the civil rights movement became the next step for the fulfillment of America's calling. The civil rights movement also included fulfilling the nation's instruction through prophecy to join church (meaning the power of religion, not one particular denomination) and government to promote and realize justice and freedom.

Martin Luther King referred to America's heritage, just as did the abolitionists, to arouse the American conscience and consciousness to do what was right. Many churches led the way to initiate social and political justice in fulfillment of the original covenant that united church and state in instituting and guaranteeing justice. King's speeches and writings reminded Americans of their accountability to their constitution and their Judeo-Christian roots. He knew that freedom and justice were built into the fabric of our nation's character. The most important threads of our fabric, the ones that were at the heart of our identity, had to do with freedom and justice.

When King called upon our Constitution and its principles to support his arguments for the end of segregation, he was following the traditions of his forefathers—not his African forefathers, but his Puritan forefathers. Slavery may have begun in the colonies in 1619, but the ideas and beliefs that would end slavery were also present at that time. The covenant God made with the Pilgrims—and ten years later with the Puritans—set the nation on a course that would guarantee freedom and justice for all. The war between the two ideas—slavery and freedom—began when the nation was founded. The godly principles of freedom and justice had to be victorious and they were.

King revealed the power of those godly ideas when he gave his "I Have a Dream" speech in Washington, D.C., on August 28. He rooted his argument in America's heritage of freedom:

> In a sense we have come to our nation's capital to cash a check. When the architects of our republic wrote the magnificent words of the Constitution and the Declaration of Independence, they were signing a promissory note to which every American was to fall heir. This note was a promise that all men would be guaranteed the inalienable rights of life, liberty, and the pursuit of happiness.
>
> It's obvious today that America has defaulted on this promissory note insofar as her citizens of color are concerned. Instead of honoring this sacred obligation, America has given the Negro people a bad check which has come back marked "insufficient funds." But we refuse to believe that the bank of justice is bankrupt. We refuse to believe that there are insufficient funds in the great vaults of opportunity of this nation. So we have come to cash this check—a check that will give us upon demand the riches of freedom and the security of justice. We have also come to this hallowed spot to remind America of the fierce urgency of now. This is no time to engage in the luxury of cooling off or to take the tranquilizing drug of gradualism. Now is the time to rise from the dark and desolate valley of segregation to the sunlit path of racial justice. Now is the time to open the doors of opportunity to all of God's children.

Now is the time to lift our nation from the quicksands of racial injustice to the solid rock of brotherhood.

King developed the same idea in his last speech, titled "I See the Promised Land":

Now we've got to go on to Memphis just like that. I call upon you to be with us Monday. Now about injunctions: We have an injunction and we're going into court tomorrow morning to fight this illegal, unconstitutional injunction. All we say to America is, "Be true to what you said on paper." If I lived in China or even Russia, or any totalitarian country, maybe I could understand the denial of certain basic First Amendment privileges, because they hadn't committed themselves to that over there. But somewhere I read of the freedom of assembly. Somewhere I read of the freedom of speech. Somewhere I read of the freedom of the press. Somewhere I read that the greatness of America is the right to protest for right. And so just as I say, we aren't going to let any injunction turn us around. We are going on. [8]

And also in the speech in Detroit, he refers again to our heritage:

Almost one hundred and one years ago, on September the 22nd, 1862, to be exact, a great and noble American, Abraham Lincoln, signed an executive order, which was to take effect on January the first, 1863. This executive order was called the Emancipation Proclamation and it served to free the Negro from the bondage of physical slavery. But one hundred years later, the Negro in the United States of America still isn't free. [Applause]

But now more than ever before, America is forced to grapple with this problem, for the shape of the world today doesn't afford us the luxury of an anemic democracy. The price that this nation must pay for the continued oppression and exploitation of the Negro or any other minority group is the price of its own destruction. For the hour is late. The clock of destiny is ticking out, and we must act now before it's too late. (Yeah) [Applause][9]

Clearly, as revealed by the speeches above, King understood and depended upon the Judeo-Christian principles that guaranteed rights to all citizens of America. He depended upon those principles and the consciences of Americans to complete the legal reforms to expand those rights to African Americans and other minorities. If he had lived in Russia or China or any other country whose government was not founded on Judeo-Christian and Western principles, he would not have succeeded. He would have been killed or jailed for the rest of his life. Our heritage is the source for our ongoing and continuous movement toward justice.

As we can see from our recent history of the civil rights movement, America's destiny continues to guide our nation to this day even in the midst of the Culture War and the antithetical consequences of the Cultural Revolution. We have not been able to escape our destiny; however, it becomes increasingly difficult to remain true to our calling. Plus, the country has been divided and confused by the constant cultural battles. The antichrist system of socialism, communism, or progressivism, whatever to call it, continues to persist in replacing Judeo-Christian principles with secular ones.

Most citizens don't understand the strife in Congress and politics. They sense a moral conflict within our culture and realize the problems when raising their children, wanting to protect them from the rampant immorality in the media and often in the schools. However, they still don't understand its source. They have lost the moral compass of absolutes, which have been replaced by the moral relativism of secular humanism. The majority may never understand it. Explanations and exposure will not win the battles of the Culture War. Only by believers reentering institutions of influence and reintroducing the Judeo-Christian ideas and principles upon which our nation was founded can we win the Culture War.

Personal Experience

When I was in high school, during the 1950s, and heard and saw in the news the injustices against American blacks, I believed in God's plan for America and the principles of equality and freedom. During my teenage years, I was passionate about politics and our national responsibility for justice. I was raised without an experience of racial prejudice although I was deeply moved by the plight of blacks in the South. In the summer between my sophomore and junior year at college, a friend and I decided to live and work in Baton Rouge, Louisiana. We wanted to acquire first-hand knowledge of the state and the condition of blacks in the South. We had not thought about joining any of the civil rights movements, but we wanted experience and understanding of conditions of injustice.

It was the summer of 1960. We arrived in Baton Rouge and found jobs as waitresses near Louisiana State University. The cooks were black and the family who owned the restaurant were Italian. The relationship appeared pleasant and agreeable, but the possibility for advancement and improvements for the black employees was non-existent. The cook, a woman, was very intelligent and an excellent cook. You could see the intelligence and poise in her eyes and in the way she carried herself. She knew she was smarter and more talented than her bosses, but she held back any superior attitudes. She wasn't subservient, but she also didn't reveal her confidence or her self-assurance.

The owners were planning to expand their business by marketing her recipe for crawfish bisque. She would not receive any compensation for the recipe or product. The owners had no consciousness of the disrespect and disregard revealed in their plans. If someone had confronted them, accusing them of being unfair, they would not have comprehended their injustice. It would not have computed in their brains that she should receive recognition and compensation for her creation. It was just the way things were done in the South at that time. Blacks were invisible. Their accomplishments could never receive equal rewards and recognition to whites because the southern culture saw blacks as inferior and less human.

My friend and I drove through the black areas near the restaurant. They had dirt roads and houses that were just thrown together. Not all African Americans lived that way in the South, but in that part of Baton Rouge, I felt their hopelessness when I drove through the black community. Many houses had an expensive car, usually a Cadillac, parked in front and TV antennas on their warped roofs, yet if the house burned down, it could be rebuilt in a day. They were just shacks. Their cars and television gave them self-respect and the respect of their neighbors because they could not improve their homes. I didn't really get involved by joining the civil rights movement, but the experience deepened my sympathy and empathy for anyone who is mistreated for being a minority.

The Twenty-First Century

This new century exploded on September 11, 2001. Having defeated antichrists and antichrist systems in the twentieth century, we were now confronted with another antichrist system—radical Islam. Osama Bin Laden and President Ahmadinejad in Iran fall into the category of antichrists because they have universal visions for purifying and cleansing the world. Bin Laden's attack on America's symbolic buildings ended a short reprieve from fighting antichrists.

America had a ten-year rest before it was thrown back into its destiny and calling. Al-Qaeda and all radical Muslims threaten to strip freedom from all the people and nations they can conquer. In all ages, the spirit of antichrist reappears in creative forms to constantly fight against God's principles and plan. America, again, has stepped into the role of the warrior against evil. Not that we are perfect. We have failed to be that City on a Hill for other religious people in this world. Our moral collapse has undermined our godly reflection. However, God has continued to answer our prayers and has used us to fight His battles.

The Fulfillment of God's Calling for a New Kind of Government

Besides fulfilling the call to fight antichrists, support Israel, and be a model of a Christian nation, America was challenged to accomplish some of its other spiritual goals during the twentieth century. From the time of the first Puritans, God instructed them to create a new kind of government in America that promised equality and freedom to all its citizens. Later, our Constitution reflected the increased knowledge of God's plan for governments throughout the world. He wanted governments to provide equality and freedom to their citizens. It's God's nature to re-create what He values and what represents His own nature. Because the Father, Son, and Holy Spirit are equal—so also God worked through history to provide equality for his human children. God established "equal justice under the law."

God also promised freedom, not just freedom from spiritual bondage, but also freedom from government enslavement. He revealed to the Founding Fathers that He was the source for human rights. Freedom of religion, speech, press, assembly, and redress from government were only a few of the many freedoms God guaranteed. The spread of freedom and equality became an expansion of God's calling on America to create a new kind of government.

In the twentieth and twenty-first centuries, America has increased its fulfillment and expansion of this new kind of government offering freedom and equality. It helped Germany and Japan become democracies after World War II and helped other nations throughout the world to embrace democracy. The recent effort in Iraq was part of America's goal to spread democracy and with it freedom and equality in the Middle East. The Iraq War and final result appear to have accomplished that goal, and it may begin a movement toward democracy throughout the Middle East.

The difficulty in promoting democracy is that without moral restraints in the people, and checks and balances in the government, democracy can become anarchy, rather than freedom and egalitarianism, instead of equality. Democracy is not a panacea to achieve God's will for a new kind of government. Without certain legal and moral limitations, it can become a source for the opposite of God's goal. In a democracy, individualism can lead to willful self-gratification, undermining the morals and self-discipline of the majority. It can become the means for a demagogue to deceive the people into losing the very freedom and equality it promises to provide.

God helped our founders create a republican form of democracy and placed the power in the hands of a morally informed people. His formula for democracy guarantees freedom and equality.

We have deviated from His formula and only have a certain amount of time to restore its original structure.

The move to socialism in this country is the opposite of God's plan. Socialism causes the people to put their trust in the state instead of in God. Socialism is anti-God and anti-family. It wants to create a people dependent upon government, rather than create a people with stable families producing stable, intelligent children who can exercise power justly. In God's plan, the people use the state to preserve freedom and equality; the state doesn't use the people to support and build up its power.

We are presently in a battle for our republic and our democracy. If an all-encompassing government becomes the source for our rights, these rights can be lost through the decision of some bureaucrat or politician. Walk carefully, America. Do not forget your prophetic calling to create a government that depends upon religion to guide and protect it. Our rights come from God and so religion is part of our government. Without God-focused religion, we will no longer have democracy. It provides our rights and our moral compass. Without either of them, we will be one more empire destroyed by internal corruption that gives away its freedom for the promise of material self-gratification.

The Fulfillment of God's Calling to Cleanse the Churches

The goal to cleanse the churches from false doctrines has been ongoing throughout the twentieth century. The practice of disgruntled members starting new churches whenever they saw their leadership fall into error has always been a practice in the United States.

The goal of holiness and perfection has been a strain of influence throughout America's religious history. The abolition movement rose out of that strain. The holiness ideas continue to survive in our culture, but they are less accepted and practiced. For our churches and Christians to be able to achieve the fullness of the Gentiles, as understood by the Puritans, it will take some soul-searching by the body of Christ in our country. Not that we will return to the holiness of the past, but we can move into achieving the holiness God has placed in our reach: one that grabs and cleanses our hearts, removing the core sins and addictions that make us slaves to Satan. God wants His children to live moral lives. He wants them to not only sacrifice for His kingdom but also to be obedient. The culture fights against holiness and morality, causing many believers to practice the corrupt ways of the world.

Francis Schaeffer wrote *A Christian Manifesto* in 1981 in which he described a new way, a humanist way, in which the general public and many Christians think. "Dr. Schaeffer noted the fundamental 'change in the overall way people think and view the world and life as a whole. This shift has been *away from* a world view that was at least vaguely Christian in people's memory (even if they were not individually Christian) toward something completely different—toward a world view based upon the idea that the final reality is impersonal matter or energy shaped into its present form by impersonal chance.'"[10]

The idea of an impersonal force being in charge leaves even Christians questioning whether they are going to be held accountable for their sins and whether there is surely an absolute truth and code of morality that have to be followed.

Scripture speaks of Christ expecting His bride to be without spot or wrinkle. At this dark and sinful time, we are more equipped for repentance than in a time of obedience and moral courage. Because of the awareness of our failings, we can be propelled away from sin by our revulsion and shame.

God does have a plan to restore our Judeo-Christian values to our culture. God will not abandon our nation to atheists and secularists. Since 9/11, there has been a move toward greater appreciation of family and more protectiveness from immoral influences undermining the family. Many people have returned to church, and Christian influence is on the increase. It's time, God's time, for Christians to make their move. We cannot hide our light under the bushel. The Holy Spirit can restore Judeo-Christian principles to the culture if we are willing to participate in His plan. We are called to return to the culture and use our God-inspired and magnified talents to impress and influence those important institutions that manipulate our culture and determine our value system.

The next chapter begins the instructions on what is required to take back our country and restore its original values. God is calling for Culture Warriors, as Bill O'Reilly calls them. It will take warriors, and they will have to be trained and supported. Churches and Christian schools and colleges will be a source for the training and support. It is the job of the body of Christ to prepare warriors to withstand the temptations and intellectual attacks they will encounter in their missionary efforts to our fallen culture.

Let us join God in the trenches, returning to the institutions we abandoned out of fear, beginning in the 1940s. We have suffered because of our failures. We're like the Israelites, too fearful to do battle in the Promised Land. Let us leave the wilderness. There are no giants. They are only shadows of a lie. Let us get ready to take back the land—it's our inheritance. Our nation belongs to God, and we are His servants and soldiers. Let us live up to the prophetic calling for our nation, and allow our churches to complete the fullness of the Gentiles by doing justly, living righteously, being courageous, and pleasing God.

CHAPTER SIX

Restoration:
The Role of Churches

There was a nation, an "island" in the midst of oceans, which shone brightly among all nations. It was not perfect but had a heart for perfection, looking to win favor with God. It provided a home for the destitute, persecuted, and poor. This nation created the first government by the people and fought a civil war—citizen against citizen—to establish freedom and equality for all. It never stopped in its pursuit to improve justice and mercy for its entire people. It reached outside its boundaries to fight and defeat evil men and systems, which were threatening the existence of other nations.

God's values ruled the hearts and minds of this nation's people and guided their institutions. The nation's many churches taught of God's principles and His laws, keeping the people in constant awareness of His expectations. He blessed them because of their covenant with Him and their efforts to please Him. He built a hedge around them to protect them from evil nations and leaders who wanted to destroy His model of charity and goodness.

Now there was a day when the angels came and presented themselves before God, and Satan also came before Him. God asked Satan where he had been.

Satan answered, "I have been traveling to and fro across the earth and walking upon it."

God said to Satan, "Have you seen My nation, America? There is no nation like her. Her people honor My name and follow My laws as their own. She fears Me and teaches her children to fear Me."

Satan answered, "I have seen Your beloved nation, America. Its people only serve You because You have blessed and protected them from the tragedies and evil that inflict other nations. If You lowered Your hedge and let her encounter the evil thoughts, lusts, and lawlessness penetrating other nations, she would turn to me and become mine. If You allowed her hopes and innocence to be dashed, she would turn away from You. She would curse You."

The Lord answered Satan, "You may attack America's morals, her leaders, and her faith in Me, but you may not defeat her using the power of other nations. You will see that even though she stumbles she will not fall. She belongs to Me."

Satan left God's presence and began his assault upon America. (Conversation based upon chapter one of the book of Job.)

The period for the beginning of Satan's assault began in the 1960s. On reflection, I believe that God allowed Satan to release demons from the pit of hell to test and refocus our nation. The sixties felt as if a volcano of demons ascended onto the earth, this time including America, and challenged the faith of those who called themselves Christians. The demons saw a generation ready to throw off its traditions and values and strike out against the foundational principles that gave America its identity. America had seen itself as a Christian nation or, at least, as a nation founded and built on Christian principles. Yet, it stumbled quickly at the roar of demonic temptations. We were tested and definitely found wanting.

With thousands of churches in the United States and millions of citizens identified as Christians, how was it possible that by the end of the 1960s the Enemy could capture the sexual and sensual pulse of our culture and then expand his reach into our hearts and minds? The Enemy thrust himself into American culture in the 1960s, but the fullness of his reach took another forty years. It began with free love, drugs, and anger at the establishment and end with a secular culture.

Where were the churches during these times? They were supposed to be the strongholds of righteousness and biblical principles. Why were they not able to prevent the Cultural Revolution? We need to know how God's shepherds failed to protect the sheep. What was missing and how can pastors and church leadership correct the weaknesses in the churches? Churches can play a role in its restoration if the leadership in the various denominations chooses to seek reform.

MAINLINE CHURCHES

Personal Experience

It was in the summer of 1952. I was twelve years old and filled with love for Jesus. I had met the Lord at a Campus Crusade retreat in the mountains of Southern California. I returned to my home in Laguna Beach with great enthusiasm, hoping to grow in my new-found faith. I anxiously came back to my local Presbyterian church, looking for spiritual food, but something was missing. My pastor gave sermons that "tickled the ears" of his congregation. Since most of the members didn't want conviction for sin, the pastor presented them ways to feel good about themselves without having to search their hearts or stop sinning.

I didn't know it at the time, but my pastor was not a born-again Christian. He had gone the way of many mainline pastors by the 1950s. He had traded the gospel for a social gospel and intellectual pride. He had already succumbed to the socialist plan: "Infiltrate the churches and replace revealed religion with social religion. Discredit the Bible and emphasize the need for intellectual maturity, which does not need a religious crutch."[1]

Social gospel ideas began to surface at the end of the nineteenth century and opened the way for the twentieth century progressive, socialist ideas to discredit the Bible. The social gospel ideas united with an intellectual and social approach to Christianity. They included certain branches of Methodist, Presbyterian, Episcopalian, and Lutheran denominations. They encompassed a definite movement toward liberal ideas. "Such were the forces which now began to challenge the church and there soon emerged a new type of church leadership, as a result, which advocated not only the promoting of charity but also the furthering of economic justice."[2]

It was not the concern for society and justice that contradicted God's goals. God cares about justice and wants people to experience justice. If Christians see injustice, they cannot turn away and do nothing. The Good Samaritan reveals a Christian's responsibility to help the oppressed. God's view of social justice was misinterpreted by those who developed the ideas of social justice. They took it beyond God's plan and created a faulty doctrine.

When pastors provide their congregation with a social gospel that plays down the importance of holiness and traditional values, they are leading them down a shallow, lukewarm path. Where the evangelicals emphasized excesses in emotion, the mainline churches gravitated to intellectual liberalism. Similar to liberal courts with the Constitution, they felt the Bible needed to be modernized and reinterpreted according to the social needs of society. The response to needs of the poor, oppressed, and underprivileged became the litmus test for Christian behavior. The mainline denominations became self-righteous because of their good works, tending to neglect and deemphasize the need for obedience to Jesus' moral teachings. When pastors make their members feel superior and righteous because they know the real truth of the Bible and give to the poor or say they care about the underprivileged, while sinning in many other ways, they are letting them live in deception.

The pastoral leaders in the abolitionist and civil rights movements didn't limit the gospel to creating a social utopia on this earth. They didn't put justice before salvation, but they revealed that justice followed from salvation. When a person is born again, he or she has a conscience informed by God and His Scriptures. As a result of the knowledge of right from wrong, a Christian cannot sit by and allow injustice to thrive. For example, he cannot let his neighbor be lynched without intervening.

Those who created the social gospel became more enamored with social justice at the sacrifice of the salvation goal and message. However, even more insidious was its mixing Christian doctrine with a rising pessimism and intellectual questioning that put the inspiration of the Scriptures in question. Intellectual sophists confused religious leaders with their progressive ideas; they confused the priority of Christ's message. They reversed the order for societal justice, making it precede individual commitment to Christ.

Many mainstream Protestant leaders changed the interpretation of the Word of God to fit their need for intellectual superiority. They fell into this elitist trap because intellectual and secular elites pressured religious leaders by humiliating them for accepting God's Word at face value. They were berated for being simple-minded and unsophisticated if they accepted the stories of Jonah and Noah's Ark as fact and not myths. The theology is much more complicated than I can describe here since this book is not the place to enter that conversation. Suffice it to say that it was the sinful pride involved in these pursuits that caused these churches to fail to prepare their members for the socialist attack on our culture.

The religious elite also began to exercise authority from the top down. They didn't concentrate on serving their congregations but on dominating and manipulating their minds with watered-down doctrine. They wanted the respect of the world and inverted God's model for exercising authority. In the worldly model, those with the greatest authority possess the greatest power and influence. The religious elites—modern liberal Pharisees—emulated their intellectual, worldly brethren as they imposed or at least imparted false doctrines to their congregations.

Personal Experience

My friend Marcia and I regularly studied the Bible together while we attended the University of California at Santa Barbara. We were very dedicated to God's Word and were committed to understanding it. Somehow we were invited to attend a special event at a mainline denomination seminary in Marin County. I can't remember the details of that event, but I remember Marcia and I were excited about being around other Christians, especially those called to the ministry. We expected to have uplifting, spiritual conversations with men and women who loved the Scriptures and were seeking understanding.

Were we shocked when we found out that our conversations with the seminarians ended up in arguments about what they called the many myths in the Bible! Here we were, two girls from a public university, arguing with seminarians about the truth of the Bible. We were terribly disappointed, but we didn't understand how secular ideas and intellectual superiority were infiltrating the seminaries of the mainline denominations at the time. We thought it was just a disappointing day involving one unique situation. It was not, though! Many mainline denominations were already being caught in intellectual elitism.

God allowed the kingdom of the world to become more dominant in mainline churches during the beginning of the socialist and secular era, weakening their contribution to their spiritual calling as described by the Puritans. They became lukewarm Christians in the 1940s and 1950s and fell into the elitist trap that undermined and demoralized all of God's instruments throughout history. Intellectual pride—whether in churches or societies—corrupts the institutions that are supposed to retain the integrity and godliness of a people. That is why Paul warned:

> Where *is* the wise? Where *is* the scribe? Where *is* the disputer of this age? Has not God made foolish the wisdom of this

world? For since, in the wisdom of God, the world through wisdom did not know God, it pleased God through the foolishness of the message preached to save those who believe. For Jews request a sign, and Greeks seek after wisdom; but we preach Christ crucified, to the Jews a stumbling block and to the Greeks foolishness, but to those who are called, both Jews and Greeks, Christ the power of God and the wisdom of God. Because the foolishness of God is wiser than men, and the weakness of God is stronger than men. (1 Cor. 1:20–25)

All ages have their Pharisees and Sadducees, the self-righteous religious elite. The Pharisees and Sadducees caused Judaism to fall into error and ineffectiveness. They used their intellects to twist God's Word and promote their own ways. The hierarchy in the Roman Catholic Church also fell into the same sins during the Middle Ages, leading to the Reformation. Yes, the Protestant Reformation stripped away much of the hierarchy that sponsored pride, selfish ambition, and dominance, but even so, lingering vestiges of human wisdom were still on the surface. For that reason, the Lord sent the Puritans to New England to cleanse out the elitist, intellectual challenge to God's ways. However, in the twentieth century the mainline denominations in the United States yielded to the same temptation as previous religious intelligentsia and felt the need to sophisticate Christ's message. That is why Paul warned further,

For you see your calling, brethren, that not many wise according to the flesh, not many mighty, not many noble, *are called*. But God has chosen the foolish things of the world to put to shame the wise, and God has chosen the weak things of the world to put to shame the things which are mighty; and the base things of the world and the things which are despised God has chosen, and the things which are not, to bring to nothing the things that are, that no flesh should glory in His presence. But of Him you are in Christ Jesus, who became for us wisdom from God—and righteousness and sanctification and redemption—that, as it is written, *"He who glories, let him glory in the* LORD.*"* (1 Cor. 1:26–31)

EVANGELICAL CHURCHES

The mainline churches fell short of God's plan because of intellectual pride, but there were other Christians who didn't fall into this trap. They were the fundamentalists, Pentecostals, and holiness Christians, referred to here as evangelicals. Most of these Christians didn't accept the elitist approach. They appealed to a person's heart to accept Christ as personal Savior. However, the emphasis on emotion and feeling and the so-called neglect of the intellect became a weakness over a period of time. They are and were part of the American tradition of Christians who mainly avoided the world and its intellectual aspects. The evangeliecals taught and emphasized the need to avoid involvement in the "things of this world." They emphasized emotion over the intellect and created a bias in many Christian denominations against participating in the intellectual marketplace of American life.

Many scholars and historians think the move away from approaching Christian teaching through reason to the emphasis of appealing to emotion occurred during two spiritual movements in early America, the First Great Awakening in the 1730s and 1740s and the Second Great Awakening from 1790 to the 1840s. The Great Awakenings broke with Puritan tradition.

The Puritans were very well read and believed strongly in the use of reason to verify Christian truths, although they were open to spiritually animated prophetic utterances as seen in Edward Johnson's history. They believed in order and a somewhat traditional class system but without a noble class. The Puritan pastors and leaders were distressed when the first Great Awakening turned emotional. They resisted its extremes; however, its excesses were caused by the circumstances beyond their control. Most of the new settlers were not Puritans or Pilgrims. They were poor, uneducated people seeking a better life, living some distance from each other on homesteaded land. The Awakenings helped to bring those new immigrants to salvation, but colonial society lost the order and rationalism of the first colonists.

Not that the Great Awakening was totally unproductive. The two Great Awakenings were a source and inspiration for both the

Revolutionary War and Civil War. As revealed in chapter three, most abolitionists were motivated by a sense of justice founded upon their Christian beliefs. In addition, the twentieth century had its share of spiritual revivals in the tradition of the Great Awakenings—Billy Graham's revivals, the Jesus and charismatic movements, and the mega-church movement being examples. However, in the twentieth century this approach did not succeed in the war against socialism. We could use some of the insights of our early ancestors.

Although the Puritans and Pilgrims didn't emphasize emotion, they did open the door for an excess of individualism and personal expression when they pushed for an even greater cleansing than other Protestant reformers from the Roman Catholic doctrines of central control, unified sacramental practices, and orderly traditions. The Puritans and Pilgrims in America went further than early Protestant reformers in cleansing and separating themselves from the Roman traditions and scholarship that had defended the faith with their theological systems of thought. Nancy Pearcey in her book *Total Truth* explains, "It was the Reformation that first introduced the new theme—the idea that the past was a morass of corruption and that the true church could be found only by throwing out centuries of historical development to recover an earlier, purer pattern."[3] As a consequence of their criticisms of Roman Catholic practices, Protestants ended up "denouncing creeds, confessions, ceremonies and ecclesiastical structures as violations of Christian liberty that must be stripped away."[4] They looked to the Bible and early church model without the intellectual and rational traditions of the fathers of the church. Without the intellectual apologetics developed by early church thinkers, over time, Christians were left without the intellectual tools to refute scientific, philosophical, and secular falsehoods.

Personal Experience

In 1971, my husband and I finally made enough money to escape San Francisco and the poor area in which we lived. The Fillmore area was being redeveloped, and many of the pimps, prostitutes, and drug dealers were moving to the area where we lived. We had two young children, and we couldn't let them grow up in the depraved Fillmore area. I prayed for God to find us a new home in a safe place for our children.

He answered my prayer by moving us to Ferndale, California, an especially beautiful little town. Being out of the hippie influence, I was desiring to find other Christians. I heard that a local store owner and his wife were Christians, so I would go into the store and hang out in the Christian book section. One day as I left the store, the owner approached me and asked if my husband and I would come to dinner at his home. That became our introduction to the Jesus Movement, which was an evangelistic outreach to hippies. I recommitted my life to the Lord and my husband found the Lord soon after.

The storeowner was a self-made and self-appointed pastor. He was formerly a police officer and through personal study, reading books and listening to tapes, he put himself into ministry. He had real charisma and many former hippies and young people were drawn into his church. He became very controlling, pressuring members to live where he designated. Emotionally starved, most members clung to him out of a need for affection and guidance from a father figure. I know my husband and I were drawn to him for that reason. He molded himself into a person many young people needed.

One time he talked to me about my university education. He said I should denounce all I had learned and turn to faith in God. He said my intellect was getting in my way of having simple faith. I needed to deny my learning and focus upon the Bible. I took his advice to heart and prayed for God to remove my intellectualism. Although over-intellectualism can interfere with faith, in this case, denying that part of myself opened me up to becoming more emotional and unstable. I cut myself off from all other literature except Christian books and the Bible. It was a form of isolation to separate me from a connection with my past and with the knowledge that would make me question him.

I followed the pastor's advice for a number of years and removed myself from my community and from unbelievers. I became an insulated Christian who helped within the church, but made little impact on the world. During the 70s, when God most needed his soldiers in the marketplace of ideas and values, I abandoned this world for the other world along with millions of other Christians. I neglected my calling to be light and salt in American culture and society.

My experience was an extreme form of the anti-intellectualism of fundamentalist Christians, but it reveals a tendency in evangelical circles that has to be corrected for us to impact the culture. We will have to produce some good minds, not just good hearts, to be able to enter and impact institutions of learning, the news media, the arts, and politics. Churches and pastors are not only called to identify and prepare those called to church ministry, but also those called to secular ministry. Christians are called to be *in the world* although *not of it.* It's time for us to be in it, to be a voice of reason and light to the intellect as well as the spirit to neutralize socialist power.

The socialist hold on American government and culture has only increased with the continued anti-intellectual and anti-rational approach of evangelicals. Some evangelical leaders, such as Jerry Falwell with the Moral Majority and Pat Robertson with the Christian Coalition, rallied Christians to action. They directed their efforts at government, but with limited success. The government was only one institution of the many that socialists had come to control. Christians could not have the same universal effectiveness as in previous centuries. Passion, emotion, and spiritual enthusiasm could not defeat this enemy. It required the dominance of Christian principles in the institutions with the most influence on people's minds.

After the 1960s, secular ideas and practices erupted and overflowed into the mainstream culture. Up until then, our Judeo-Christian traditions had held back those ideas, relegating them to a censured, artistic, liberal subculture—movie stars, artists, and beatniks. The overflow of secularism and socialism sank into the roots of our society through the institutions that had already been infiltrated by secular intellectuals who had prepared the soil, planted the seed, and now enjoyed the harvest. Christians and traditionalists were caught unawares because they had not realized what was happening and had not kept current with antichrist strategies.

While evangelical Christians withdrew from society during the beginning of the Cultural Revolution, liberals completed their infiltration of what could be described as the "brain" and "heart" of American culture. They took control of the institutions that controlled the minds and emotions of most Americans. Christians allowed radical liberals to take over the institutions of public education, unions, courts, news media, television and movies, colleges and universities, arts, music, some church denominations, and many local and state political bodies. It's not surprising that efforts to infiltrate and capture our institutions have been ongoing and very successful since many Christians unknowingly surrendered those institutions.

Many evangelicals didn't relish having to withstand rejection, ridicule, and persecution in the most influential institutions—so they surrendered their circles of influence. They withdrew to safer and less culturally significant career choices, such as commerce, business, agriculture, and medicine. These institutions remained less threatening than the others mentioned above. Their removal had the same effect as when Nebuchadnezzar either killed or kidnapped the leadership and the best and brightest in Judah in the Babylonian captivity. He knew that if he cut off the head, the body would die or at least remain passive and non-threatening. Daniel, Shadrach, Meshach, and Abed-Nego were some of the promising future leaders of Judah, and Nebuchadnezzar used them to benefit his kingdom. In the same way, many Christians were cut off from places of cultural leadership. They withdrew and were pushed out of education, the media, courts, unions, the Democrat Party, and the arts. They entered industries and careers that had some influence, but were not in those institutions that were most instrumental in preserving Judeo-Christian principles in the culture.

Evangelicals' approach to cultural warfare has been unsuccessful because they failed to keep their people current on intellectual understanding of their beliefs and moral laws, and they lost their courage in the face of better-trained opponents. The church was fighting against an enemy—socialism—that knew how to manipulate people's minds and emotions and play on people's fears. They developed methods to confuse and deceive them. The People's Organizations formed by Saul Alinsky, mentioned in chapter one, presented their goals and visions with the same religious enthusiasm as evangelicals. Then they took their message onto radio, television, movies, and now the Internet. These tools made their techniques even more powerful and influential. As you will see in chapter eight, their tactics became so refined they could and can undo and disarm Christians and conservative weapons. Even evangelical Christians became confused and confounded by the mixture of the secular deceptions with Christian teachings, such as making tolerance look like Christian love and righteous anger look like meanness.

As we have seen, since the Protestant Reformation, evangelicals withdrew from the secular, objective world to a spiritual, subjective experience of God, allowing the secularist to make great strides in redefining America's worldview. America's Christian worldview lost ground because evangelicals lost the battle for objective truth. God was felt and experienced, and it was not necessary to prove His doctrines objectively true because until the 1960s the majority of Americans didn't question Judeo-Christian values.

Once the Judeo-Christian culture and Christian beliefs were attacked, evangelicals fell into a socialist trap of fighting back with emotion rather than reason. In addition, the secular enticement for self-gratification leaned on many Christians to draw them away from their faith. Many fell away, being enticed to satisfy their sexual desires and get high on drugs. Without intellectual understanding of their faith and clear moral teachings on right or wrong, many Christians just blended in with the secular culture. God was relegated to a spiritual realm outside the culture rather than holding a place to define the culture. During the 1960s, the humanist, socialist, and secular revolutionaries won the first major battle in the Culture War.

Although many Christians have withdrawn from much of secular society, there has been a remnant making great efforts to restore our Christian heritage. There have been an energetic few, and they have achieved some notable successes. The Moral Majority and Christian Coalition made strides in the 1980s, and Christian television has had a positive influence. In fact, the salvation message has reached millions through Christian television. There are many other organizations putting most of their efforts into influencing or opposing the policies and laws of states and the federal governments. Government is only one post in our national house; it doesn't have enough influence to restore our culture to its roots. Therefore, we now need more Christians committed to fighting the Culture War with a different strategy. That strategy involves returning to all the influential institutions we abandoned and being committed for as many years as it takes to win the Culture War. Socialists have persisted for many years to accomplish their goals. Christians should be able to surpass their determination and patience.

Other Evangelical Weaknesses

The need for a long-term commitment, as mentioned above, highlights another evangelical weakness. Many evangelicals have become distracted by teachings on the End Times. Many born-again believers are certain Jesus will return in their lifetime. They have lost the vision for America by concentrating so much on preparing for Jesus' imminent return. The Lord warns against Christians trying to predict the time of His return because it paralyzes those caught up in false hope.

It is time for believers to be about the Lord's business instead of trying to avoid the spiritual battles occurring in our nation. They need to make a long-term commitment to enter into the battles for as many years as required and sacrifice their own desires for their lives to God's plan for their lives as Culture Warriors.

Besides the weaknesses of concentrating too much on the End Times, the prejudice against an intellectual understanding of Christian doctrines, and a dependence on emotion, some evangelical churches have another hindrance to influencing the culture. With the advent of Christian television, a new style of preaching and leadership has emerged. Television magnifies the possibility for preachers to become powerful and famous. The ambition to achieve acclaim is a seed planted in the heart of many seminarians, even if only a few achieve that goal. The possibility to reach millions entices many pastors. Of course, their desires are couched in terms of reaching millions for Christ, and some of their ambition is guided by unselfish motives, but if selfish ambition lingers as yeast in the dough and it's not removed—it will take over the whole of those pastors' motives over time.

Not all evangelical pastors, of course, but a considerable number of them fall into this pattern. When senior pastors become driven by the desire to expand their ministry out of a motive of self-importance (normally hidden from themselves), it becomes a destructive force for many ministers in their churches. A large number of the people in these churches who want to minister will have the same motives as the pastors. The pastors will attract many people to help who are willing to volunteer or work for little compensation because they have a sense of self-importance and an unrealistic idea of how God wants to use them in ministry.

Self-centered pastors are able to manipulate volunteers and underpaid staff. They can play on some of their members' desires for greatness and influence to entice them to volunteer to help in ministry or even to become paid staff. As time goes on, many of these people become disgruntled because they don't experience the rewards they expected. Also, if they don't give the expected time and energy to the ministry, they are demoted to lesser tasks, and eventually they will be replaced by another overly ambitious person. These conflicts result in constant replacements of leadership in ministry since people fall in and out of favor or reach a point of exhaustion that makes it necessary for them to stop.

The consequence of the problem above is the failure of churches to have the people called and gifted by God to help with ministry. Every church needs those volunteers God calls to pick up some of the ministering a church can't afford. When the ambitious rather than the servants take on these ministries, the church members seeking meaty teachings in those ministries will not grow. Eventually, they will become dissatisfied and disinterested and quit coming.

In some way, many of the people attracted to a church with a selfishly ambitious pastor are attracted out of a need to feel important as well. Since the 1960s, part of the socialist strategy has been to make people feel very important. The self-esteem movement in the schools is an example of that trend. Also, since many in our society have been raised in dysfunctional and abusive homes, they are very needy for a sense of importance and purpose. That is why individualism is so strong in our society. People put their own needs and excessive demands before the good of society. In order to grow in holiness, every Christian at some point in their walk has to look at the area of the heart where selfish ambition or pride dwells and ask the Lord for cleansing.

In addition, every minister, paid or volunteer, has to come to the place of death to self when it comes to ministry. Some of those who never die to their selfish ambition may have been called into ministry, but they can never be used deeply and fully because of the sin in their hearts. The biggest drawback for someone trying to minister is that they can only copy someone following the Holy Spirit; they cannot follow the Spirit themselves. If they are told to listen to the Spirit, it makes them anxious. It's difficult for them to remain quiet in prayer while the Holy Spirit guides them. They jump in when they should not and give faulty advice and practice misdirected prayers.

Personal Experience

It was one year after my husband became a Christian. He was crying and confessing some sins at a meeting when the pastor told him God wanted him to be an elder, violating the Scripture that warns against making a young convert an elder. At that moment, my husband's spiritual growth ended. He had to perform the role of an elder and deny any of his faults. The title became a burden, not a blessing.

Later, one of the members prophesied over him that he was going to be an evangelist. Anyone with any sense knew he was not called to be an evangelist. He didn't have the gifts, talents, or abilities for the calling. However, that was the disorder and dysfunction of many of the ministries that arose in the Jesus Movement.

The Jesus Movement began at the end of the 1960s as the Christian response to the hippie movement. Many hippies began to burn themselves out with drugs and sex. Their lives were turned upside down by the drug and free love culture. My husband and I were some of those lost hippies, open to God when we moved up to northern California.

I had known the Lord since I was twelve, but without Christian fellowship and pastoral guidance, I had fallen into confusion and sin. My husband was a practicing Roman Catholic, and so was I at that time. However, after some spiritual searching, we joined a church in Ferndale with a self-made pastor. I am certain his motives were somewhat pure in the beginning, but he was a young Christian and took on more than his maturity and motives could handle. One of his greatest techniques for controlling this small group of seekers was to play on their insecurities and need to feel important.

He gained control of my husband's loyalty and the loyalty of many other men through the same method as described above. He would attract the men to serve him and the ministry without pay by leading them to believe they were called to a very important ministry, probably with one of the five-fold ministry callings of apostle, prophet, pastor, teacher, and evangelist. The different callings were doled out among the men, and the women were drawn in with different enticements.

Although many of the instabilities and lawless practices of the Jesus Movement have subsided, the dysfunctions from the Cultural Revolution begun in the 1960s continue to make people very vulnerable to the need of feeling important. As mentioned above, the advent of television ministries and the increased ability through technology to reach millions has fed into this weakness.

The solution to this problem is for pastors to first have the Lord cleanse their own motives for ministry, being cleansed of selfish ambition and a desire for power and fame. It's so easy to accept the lie from Satan that God has a great work, something enormous and influential for you. God allows some preachers to reach powerful positions, even those with mixed motives, but He is looking for the true servants who look only to please Him without expectations of notoriety or power.

Pastors who have experienced cleansing and decrease should then provide spiritual teaching for their staff and volunteers to receive the same training. Everyone in ministry has to deal with the temptation of selfish ambition. It's part of human nature to desire importance, and it's absolutely necessary to deal with that weakness and sin from the very beginning and repeatedly as a person ministers. It's not a onetime event but occurs repeatedly, but there has to be an initial awareness and cleansing. If not resolved, it prevents any church from helping its members grow into mature Christians. People cannot grow if those ministering to them are too full of themselves to hear the Spirit. When leaders are *free* of selfish ambition, then they are able to lead people into maturity, teaching them to depend upon the Lord rather than keeping them dependent upon those ministering to them.

The problem above is not just an evangelical phenomenon. It exists in all churches; however, with the evangelicals' greater use of television, it has grown into a more prominent problem. It has weakened the effectiveness of many evangelical churches that had the potential for extensive and thriving ministries. God often "pulls the plug" just as a church appears triumphant. In contrast, the Roman Catholic Church has fewer temptations in this area because of their more hierarchical approach to ministry.

ROMAN CATHOLIC CHURCH

At the present the Catholic Church has returned to its conservative, traditional roots, but during the 1960s it was swept up into much of the socialist revolution. Pope John XXIII opened the church to make some changes. He discerned that the church had stagnated and needed to catch up with the modern world; therefore, he called Vatican II. Vatican II began the process of opening up the Catholic

Church to the idea of broader collegial power, removing Latin from the Mass, modernizing religious clothing, and becoming more ecumenical. It triggered unintended consequences. Liberals in the church used the changes as an opportunity to push for their agendas. The opening was too broad, and too many radical ideas began to dominate in parishes in different countries.

Some of Vatican II had a very positive effect for the Catholic Church, but it did allow for a time of increased secularization of its religious and lay members. The Catholic Church in America is now in the process of restoring correct moral and doctrinal thinking. That is why some Bishops in the U.S. have told priests to deny communion to politicians who have voted for abortion. The conservative restoration also brought out many Catholics against President Obama speaking at Notre Dame and receiving an honorary degree. The Catholic Church has often been more of a voice against the secularization of America than most Protestant churches. The Roman church has sent its members into the important institutions, the Supreme Court being one of the most important.

The weakness in the Catholic Church is its inability to communicate its messages to its members. Most lay Catholics don't understand the deep concerns of the Pope for the rights of the unborn, the importance of all life, and other doctrines. The ideas are not successfully communicated from the top to the bottom. The voting patterns of many Catholics in the United States contradict Catholic teaching. Some of the problem is that Catholic teaching appeals mainly to the mind, and their problem is the reverse of evangelicals. They need to appeal more fully to the heart and reach more of their members for Christ. Then the Holy Spirit can confirm the teachings of the Church and convict its members to follow the moral teachings of the Church.

Personal Experience

While attending college in Santa Barbara, I didn't have a car or other means to attend any local churches. Therefore, as I mentioned above, I mainly spent time in Bible study and prayer with my friend,

Marcia. I would probably have gone to a mainstream church anyway, which may not have done me much good. Since I didn't receive any teaching from pastors, I tried to read and study spiritual books. I had taken a comparative religion class and discovered the writings of the saints and fathers of the Catholic Church. I was very impressed with *The Imitation of Christ* by Thomas A. Kempis, *The Dark Night of the Soul* by John of the Cross, and *Interior Castle* by Teresa of Avila. After reading these books and discovering the spiritual journey of the soul, I had a hunger for more of the Lord. Since I had little Protestant influence, I decided to convert to Catholicism to satisfy my spiritual hunger.

I also decided to enter a convent to totally dedicate my life to Christ. In 1964, I entered the novitiate of the Immaculate Heart of Mary order, whose headquarters and college were in Hollywood. I planned to be a teacher at its college. I spent two years at the novitiate. I loved community living and the relationships I formed with other postulants and novices. However, over time I discovered that the girls dedicating their lives to Christ didn't know Him personally. It was a religious act, rather than a spiritual one, for the majority. It made me feel separated from the girls and the superiors, and it began to add to some of my other doubts about remaining in the order.

Since it was in the 1960s, it was, of course, a time of upheaval in religious communities just like everywhere else. Vatican II was meeting, and its changes were already having an effect. We were told we would no longer wear full habits, we had to keep our own names rather than take the name of a saint in the church, and the Mass was now said partly in English. I was a little disappointed at the changes, but being young, I adjusted.

Even though I was happy in the novitiate, I began to feel some strain over the changes. We had a very artistic and intellectual group of sisters who had definite liberal leanings. They came in conflict with the more conservative sisters because they wanted more freedom. In a few years, the conflict led to a split in the order. The more liberal sisters became lay sisters, and the others remained under the traditional Catholic authority. The tension and split caused great distress for many of those whose lives were touched by the sisters, especially the students. I found myself in the middle of another clash of cultures, and in the end, I left the order and went in search for where I felt I belonged and where I could find more of Christ.

My life's journey traveled on the edge and in the middle of various liberal movements. I encountered the socialistic agenda in my Presbyterian Church, at the university, in the convent, as a hippie, in some aspects of the Jesus Movement, in politics in San Jose, and in the churches. We have all been touched by it, but many times people are not aware of the influence. The Lord allowed me to walk in the midst of the culture and experience its changes first hand, although He always pulled me back from embracing the deceptions.

Responsibility of Churches

From the information above it's clear that the mainline, evangelical, and Catholic churches contained flaws that kept them from doing God's will for American society, allowing God's principles to be removed from our society and culture. They have to overcome their flaws and achieve God's goals to send agents of restoration into the places of power taken over by socialists.

How are they flawed? Most of the churches in the categories above don't think that culture matters. They are interested in growing their membership, increasing salvations, bringing spiritual growth to their members, but they are not training or supporting their members to influence the culture. Connecting God's plan with influencing American culture is secondary to most churches.

God cares about a nation knowing the truth and not living in lies. He cares how a nation treats its born citizens and its unborn ones. He cares about human dignity and human life. Our churches have lost the connection of their responsibilities to the nation, and since this book is directed to Americans—our churches have lost their connection to the calling of the nation of America.

The Puritans and Founding Fathers knew of this connection. They were Daniel and Joseph to our nation. They formulated laws and rights based upon the form of government and calling that God put before them. Christians are called to move into the inner circles of power. They must commit to making our nation moral and just (protecting life and liberty). Most churches in the last hundred years have become internalized and self-centered. Volunteering in the church is encouraged to the neglect of spending time impacting the world. God used Daniel and Joseph to initiate His justice and fairness in non-Jewish nations. How much more important it is to have Christians restoring and retaining God's moral laws and justice in our nation!

God created humans in His image and likeness and our governments and nations should be in agreement with His likeness, which is revealed in His laws. Our Puritan ancestors raised and educated their children to preserve their experiment in the wilderness. Our Founding Fathers insisted Americans retain their moral compass in order to hold on to the American dream—the dream of a free and just society. Today's parents and pastors have the responsibility to educate, train, and organize God's people to be Culture Warriors so they can make our nation a representative, godly nation. Of course, His warriors always have the calling to preach the gospel, introducing people to Christ, but they also have the calling to preserve the Judeo-Christian principles that assure a morally upright and just society.

God's plan moved from Abraham to Israel to the islands—the Gentiles—because He is a God of holiness and justice and His justice proceeds from the seed of Abraham throughout the earth to all nations. Nations choose to practice justice or injustice; a just nation formulates just laws. America is a nation whose rights and laws proceeded from God.

When God created the universe and the earth, He established moral laws to guide His children. Through revelation and natural laws, humans have increased in their understanding of God's justice and how it's to be dispensed in nations. It's dispensed by applying Judeo-Christian principles to society. These principles are the expression of God's moral laws. They define God's justice. God rewards nations that practice justice and punishes those who don't. Just laws agree with and derive their existence from God's moral laws.

How can God's justice be established on earth? It's through His chosen nations. God chose Israel and made a covenant that revealed the justice that was to infiltrate the nations of the earth. Many present-day Jews believe they were scattered around the earth in order to spread the influence of God's justice. Then God founded America and, in my opinion, made a covenant of lesser calling with His "shrubs in the wilderness," the Puritans and Pilgrims, to reveal further insights into the system of justice He desired to establish. He guided and inspired, first the Puritans and then the Founding Fathers, with a unique idea of establishing a republican democracy as a model for the rest of the world.

So, not only is God's goal for sinners to be saved and for churches to bring people to salvation but also to train His people on how to establish and maintain justice in American society. For example, the Declaration of Independence and the Constitution are appendages of God's moral laws. The Declaration affirms that life, liberty, and the pursuit of happiness are inalienable (never to be surrendered) rights guaranteed by God. Therefore, Americans and especially American Christians have a responsibility to preserve and fight for the preservation of those rights. *A government cannot take away rights guaranteed by God.* Hence, when the unborn or very old are put to death because the state says their lives don't matter, Christians have to refer back to the Declaration of Independence and demand that the right to life be assured and preserved. It's the role of Christians to exercise the justice demanded by the moral laws and our political documents. It's their responsibility to ensure that the state practices justice.

How do Christians influence their government and nation? First they can only establish and preserve justice in a nation by establishing and preserving justice in their own actions and lives. When justice is in people's hearts and they live justly, they are at peace and their character is ordered. It's the churches' and pastors' responsibility to teach their members moral laws and how to apply them to their lives. They must know right from wrong and practice what is right. Once their minds and lives are ordered, they can order the world with the same principles of truth.

Christians are the body of Christ, but churches are God's right arm. Churches are designated to spiritually mature the body and to disciple its members to be the light and salt in the world. Then the world or a nation, like America, will be grounded and established in Judeo-Christian principles as a result of what kind of influence their well-trained members have in the culture. The apostles and Jesus' other disciples changed the world, and the local churches prepared and instructed them in how to bring about that transformation. God wants to use churches and pastors to train His twenty-first century army. He is ready to chain the demons released in the 1960s, but we will have to do the chaining.

Protestants can fashion armor for the battle by drawing from some of the teachings of the Catholic Church. It provides its members with knowledge of moral questions having to do with abortion, social justice, and the moral laws. They stress the need to live according to principles, such as voting according to Christian principles and pursuing truth. The popes have written encyclicals to identify the false teachings from secular society. In 1995 John Paul II wrote *Evangelium Vitae* in defense of the "Value and Inviolability of Human Life." It was based upon Genesis 4:9, where Cain asks, "*Am* I my brother's keeper?" He explained how moral relativism led to excessive freedom and how what were supposed to be inalienable rights have faded into rights of the state and the majority. *Evangelium Vitae* states:

> This is what is happening also at the level of politics and government: the original and inalienable right to life is questioned or denied on the basis of a parliamentary vote or the will of one part of the people—even if it's the majority. This is the sinister result of a relativism which reigns unopposed: the "right" ceases to be such, because it's no longer firmly founded on the inviolable dignity of the person, but is made subject to the will of the stronger part. In this way democracy, contradicting its own principles, effectively moves towards a form of totalitarianism. The State is no longer the "common home" where all can live together on the basis of principles of fundamental equality, but is transformed into a tyrant State, which arrogates

to itself the right to dispose of the life of the weakest and most defenceless members, from the unborn child to the elderly, in the name of a public interest which is really nothing but the interest of one part. The appearance of the strictest respect for legality is maintained, at least when the laws permitting abortion and euthanasia are the result of a ballot in accordance with what are generally seen as the rules of democracy. Really, what we have here is only the tragic caricature of legality; the democratic ideal, which is only truly such when it acknowledges and safeguards the dignity of every human person, is betrayed in its very foundations: "How is it still possible to speak of the dignity of every human person when the killing of the weakest and most innocent is permitted? In the name of what justice is the most unjust of discriminations practised: some individuals are held to be deserving of defence and others are denied that dignity?" When this happens, the process leading to the breakdown of a genuinely human co-existence and the disintegration of the State itself has already begun.[5]

Pope John Paul II's encyclical argues from eternal and absolute truths. It provides the readers with a firm foundation for their beliefs. It's expressed with emotion, but it doesn't depend on emotion to prove its arguments. This is only one example of Catholic writings that have held onto objective truths and absolutes. Many Roman Catholic leaders and pastors are doing much to fight to restore Judeo-Christian principles. They especially fight for human dignity and the right to life. They are focused upon the culture because of societies' violation of God's laws.

Although the Roman Catholic authority is passionate in its desire and efforts to reestablish moral absolutes worldwide, it has not yet succeeded in winning over the majority of its members. It too has just begun to use the media and has not constructed a clear plan. They could draw insights from evangelicals about how to make Jesus more personal and the Bible more understandable to their members. In that case, they could draw upon a spiritual passion of their members to rally them in their high cause to restore moral absolutes to cultures throughout the world. In America, neither tradition has successfully communicated and motivated their members to understand God's great concern for our nation. He doesn't want us to stand on the sidelines and watch our nation taken over by socialists/secularists. He has a plan and we must move quickly before it's too late.

CHAPTER SEVEN

What Is the Plan to Win the Culture War?

It pleased Darius to set over the kingdom one hundred and twenty satraps, to be over the whole kingdom; and over these, three governors, of whom Daniel *was* one, that the satraps might give account to them, so that the king would suffer no loss. Then this Daniel distinguished himself above the governors and satraps, because an excellent spirit *was* in him; and the king gave thought to setting him over the whole realm. (Dan. 6:1–3)

Christian churches and pastors of every denomination are invited to be *agents of restoration* to restore Judeo-Christian principles to our culture. We are a nation built upon and receiving our identity from those principles. They must dominate and guide all aspects of our moral and political decisions. Churches can provide the training, preparation, and support to produce Christians after the model of Daniel. These Culture Warriors will penetrate and saturate the culture with Judeo-Christian principles—truths and moral absolutes—just as did Daniel, Shadrach, Meshach, and Abed-Nego. It's the responsibility of churches and pastors to produce men and women of an excellent spirit.

Recommendation to Pastors

First, I encourage pastors to bring more teachings into their sermons about absolute truth, moral laws, and moral absolutes. Their members are hungry for principles and teachings that refute the immorality of the culture. They need to be taught moral laws and how to apply them. Most Christians don't know that God created universal moral laws when He created humans, just as He created physical laws when He created the universe.

Pastors need to tell their members that just as when a person challenges the law of gravity by jumping from a high place and suffers the consequences of broken bones or death, so also in like manner, when people violate God's moral laws they will suffer certain consequences as well. If they violate God's sexual laws, such as fornication, they will suffer some or all the consequences of separation from God, diseases, self-hatred, pregnancy, guilty conscience, depression, and anxiety. Or if they lie to a friend, they will suffer separation from God, loss of trust, loss of friendship, grief, sorrow, regret, shame, and/or guilt. They need to know that consequences are certain—they definitely will happen. The consequences are the result of breaking spiritual laws.

Another example would be to focus on the unborn and the importance of life. Pastors could provide the Scriptures that reveal how God values human life and how life begins at conception. Then in the next election, they could point out to their members that in order to be morally in God's will, they should not vote for any politician who supports abortion. (The Catholic Church does make an exception if one politician is against abortion in all cases except rape and incest while the other candidate supports blanket abortions; they recommend you vote for the lesser evil).

Making a general point about voting according to principle is not the same as telling your members to vote for a particular politician. It's their responsibility to research the voting records of the candidates—their records are very available online. Will some members of the church be offended? Yes, they will. Will they leave? They might, but it's more important to preserve your members' souls by educating their consciences with the truth than to have large numbers. And it's more important to show them their responsibility to the nation and society than keep them as members. Pastors who follow this practice will have done their part to warn their members about applying moral principles to all areas of their lives, especially voting.

Moral issues need to be confronted head-on. Paul definitely confronted this problem and didn't shy away from speaking the truth. He took responsibility for the souls of his Christian children and didn't let them fall unknowingly into sin. All Christians are Culture Warriors in the sense they are light to their acquaintances and fellow employees. They can't be light in the darkness if they're filled with darkness. And when moral issues arise in their place of work, they can respond with Judeo-Christian principles as the guideline.

Programs for Training

Along with meaty sermons, pastors can train Culture Warriors by providing workshops for training their members. Saul Alinsky and his disciples in Chicago trained people for community organizing that in the end meant revolutionizing the culture. It appeared to be a small confined work of revolution, but over many years it spread throughout the nation by a few well-placed and powerful disciples.

The focus of our efforts in training *agents of restoration* will be in the workplace, not community organizing. Every job is tied to some kind of institution that can be used to impact society. The most important are those that control the minds of the people and regulate the laws. Of course the Christian community needs to begin with itself and make sure it's cleansed from worldly obstacles, leading to an inward growth of an excellent spirit.

Churches have options on how to prepare and train their members. There are two groups that will need a different approach: First, the majority of members work in a variety of jobs but not in institutions with the most influence in society. They are very important for the complete saturation of society, but in the long term, the people in the institutions that rule the high places and high culture of society are going to require more training. Culture Warriors in influential occupations, such as news journalists, university professors, and politicians, will encounter more persecution than those working in commerce or business. And members working in large cities will normally encounter more persecution than those working in the countryside. However, the majority will require some training and follow-up as well.

Culture Warriors in the Regular Armed Forces

The majority of Christians are Warriors in the regular armed forces. They will impact millions of people on their jobs. With the sermons giving guidance, the majority would do fine with a number of workshops or an eight- or ten-week course (e.g., a shortened version of this book). God has created all of us for some vocations that bring us in contact with people and institutions in the secular world.

Paul says, "For we are His workmanship, created in Christ Jesus for good works, which God prepared beforehand that we should walk in them" (Eph. 2:10). When we conform to God's workmanship and do the good works He prepared for us to do, we are then the fullness of the body of Christ. God is always working on us to fit us into His creative mold. As more of us fit into His plan and do His good works, the wheel of His kingdom is able to more powerfully intersect with the wheel of the kingdom of the world.

God's workmanship is multifaceted. God has multiple purposes for each of His children. During our lives, all Christians are members of a family as a son or daughter, and most will be members of a family as a husband or wife, parent, and relative to others. We are all students, church members, and friends. God uses us in all these relationships. He uses these relationships for our growth into His likeness and to perfect others in the body of Christ. He uses us and our good works to touch and change all the people in that circle of relationships. All our activities in these areas are very important purposes God planned beforehand. They are always the foundation and source of strength for our lives.

Another very important relationship is where people participate in specific careers or vocations. If we are attentive to His will, we can fulfill His purpose in our careers. Most of these careers are the means by which God intersects His kingdom with the kingdom of the world. Christians impact the world and the culture most powerfully when they perform the vocations for which He made us.

In church culture, a person's career has not been given the importance God wants it to be given in fulfilling His purpose for His children. Christian ideas and principles have failed to impact our culture and world because churches have failed to help Christians pursue the jobs God ordained for each one. Individuals have feared certain careers, many choosing those that seem most convenient. Although churches have taught spiritual growth principles to their members, most have not prepared people to enter the careers God has ordained for their lives. In addition, they have not provided the tools for their members to discover their ordained career or prepared them with the tools to intersect the culture with a powerful ability to change it. Most Christian youth are not focused by their church or family to impact the kingdom of this world with God's wisdom and justice. They are allowed to seek their careers as a second thought, less important than their commitment to their church.

A person's career is of great importance to God—not as important as the person's salvation, but a close second. The Lord says we will be rewarded according to our works. Careers provide many of our good works when we enter the career that is God's purpose for our life. Young Christians should be taught to pray for God's will for their profession, starting in junior high or at least at the beginning of high school. Then the Lord can begin to guide the youth to His will. Also, churches could provide or guide young people to Christian career guidance tests. There are some very excellent ones online. The church should also remind young people to be careful to avoid sins and mistakes that will keep them from jobs God called them to do. So many times young people sacrifice their future careers by getting into alcohol or drugs or end up being promiscuous and starting an unplanned family. These events prevent or slow down their fulfilling God's will for their careers.

Of course, for women, if they marry and have children, their timetable for a career is determined by the needs of their children. Some women never enter a career, but God uses them in other ways, such as in their families and volunteering in the community or church. Some women have careers before marrying and others wait until the children are grown. Some work from home while the children are young and sometimes the mother has to work full-time. All these circumstances can be fit into God's will. Through prayer and seeking God, Christian women can find how God will use them in a career or as volunteers and how he can turn to good any wrong decision made early on.

The goal is that churches can add to parental guidance by helping young people find the career God has prepared for them and to help them avoid the sin that will keep them from God's purpose. Churches can help by giving career guidance classes for their youth or older members seeking to change their careers. They can combine these classes with the information in this book that focuses on the importance of this nation in God's purpose and also train them to be Culture Warriors. They are all part of the wheel of God's kingdom, and they are necessary as the means to intersect with the kingdom of this world.

Example of God's Impact through Careers

A friend and fellow church member, Candy, shared an experience at work where she is the administrator for patient services in a local hospital. She and a few Christians who work with her prayed together that their division would have influence outside the local area. They prayed that all the staff would give the best service to patients, with the best attitude. They came up for review in a national survey with other hospitals and ended up eighth in the nation for providing the best service.

Then they needed to submit an article to win another honor. In the article, Candy bravely mentioned the prayers of her Christian co-workers and her. She also mentioned a ministry to abused women in the church. That letter will be read by many people, and if it wins top honors, it will be published and distributed broadly to hospitals throughout California. Just by a few people praying for their workplace, they have begun a much broader work.

Another friend and fellow church member, Sherri, has a similar story. She and some other Christians who work for a Mercedes-Benz dealership began to pray for their place of employment. When the recession hit, their dealership was not affected as were many others. In fact, they grew more successful with new strategies because God gave wisdom to those making policy decisions. The owner learned about their praying at some point and, even though not yet a Christian, he is making the connection between the success of his dealership and their prayers. My friends are just two examples of how Christians can impact their workplace and beyond. God's army should be outstanding in every way, so the secular world will give God's people respect for every aspect of their contribution.

Special Forces Culture Warriors

Next we want to identify the people who are in or are going to enter the powerfully influential institutions mentioned above. Those who are working or plan to work in those industries require more training. They are the *special forces* in the armed forces.

Churches and Christian colleges should develop intern programs for those who will work in the high places of power. This book could be part of the curriculum. Supplemental materials for this curriculum are already available on my Web site: www.winning theculturewarthebook.com. This Web site provides a syllabus, assignments, classroom activities, and tests for teaching the material. It could be taught for one or two semesters or quarters, dividing the chapters up accordingly. Individuals who are not part of a participating church can follow the same courses and support online.

Those churches that participate could give useful feedback as they practice the curriculum and develop some of their own materials. This book is a first attempt to turn Christians into Culture Warriors. What we need most is for pastors to use their influence to impress their members with the great importance of becoming Culture Warriors in their workplace and to enter those fields that will powerfully impact our culture.

This plan depends upon churches and pastors inspiring and training Christian youth and other members to want to become Culture Warriors. They must inspire the most talented Christians to enter the marketplace of ideas. Christians must become creative, intellectually contributing members of American society.

As a result of this training and educational course, God can guide his volunteers into the careers in which their talents will have the greatest impact on the culture. The institutions of greatest need are the news and entertainment media, the universities (as professors), public education, law, the arts, and government service—politics and government jobs. These institutions have the greatest ability to control and manipulate people's minds. Christians should use these institutions not to control people's minds but to reintroduce abandoned Judeo-Christian principles. Therefore, the most intelligent, anointed, and creative Christians should be identified and encouraged to enter careers in those fields. University professors, are some of the most influential members of our society, yet few Christians are motivated to enter major universities or pursue PhDs.

One of the goals should be to inspire some Christian students and young adults to make the grades that will open doors into the elite and Ivy League universities. They should be attending Harvard, Yale, Princeton, Stanford, and other universities of that caliber and influence, and earning PhDs and other degrees. Besides professors' influence in the classroom, they will also write for scholarly journals and participate in think tanks. These journals and think tanks have great influence on the ideas and policies created by political leaders, especially members of Congress, the news media, and the president.

Professors also have great influence in contributing to textbooks at all levels of education. These textbooks currently present a very liberal if not socialist viewpoint. They include those ideas and facts that sway students to believe in a progressive, leftist worldview. By contributing to textbooks, they have a tremendous impact on students and publishers. Intellectual assets are in the hands of secularists—American believers have been shut out.

Presently, most Christians either enter ministry, the corporate world, small business, or the military. I know a number of Christian teenagers who initially showed an interest in journalism, teaching, and politics but changed their majors to something safer once they entered college. Most of them changed their majors to computers, business, and marketing. It's not a conscious choice; it seems almost subliminal that they move toward safer careers. This behavior must not continue. American believers can no longer stay hidden for fear of persecution or because they reject intellectually challenging careers.

The Supreme Court is a model for how Christians can reintroduce the principles on which our nation was founded. Justices John Roberts, Clarence Thomas, and Samuel Alito have their roots in their Christian faith. They are all Roman Catholics. The Roman Catholic Church has remained in the intellectual marketplace of ideas. They all graduated from prestigious universities, but they resisted joining America's liberal elite. They remained true to the legal principles established in the Constitution. They have followed a strict-constructionist approach, meaning they interpret laws based upon constitutional principles rather than interpreting laws based upon personal agendas. They don't use the courts to make laws, as do judicial activists who make efforts to reformulate society through the courts.

Of course, our most creative and intellectual warriors must avoid the elite aspect of intellectualism, but they must embrace their intellect and creative talent as given them by God for a purpose. God can increase, inspire, and sharpen warriors' intellects, intuition, and creative abilities so they will stand out from other intellectuals and influencers not only because of their enhanced God-given abilities but also because of their humble servant attitudes. They can be trained to use authority through serving not dominating, as was practiced in the early colonies.

God calls all Christians to influence the culture, but He is also calling the few with the talents, intelligence, and creativity appropriate for the most influential institutions in our society. He will call them to be the best and brightest in their careers, like Supreme Court Chief Justice John Roberts. At the same time they will need the heart and attitude of sacrifice.

Christians can no longer look for the safe place to work. They have to put themselves on the front lines. Their goal is not to infiltrate or undermine the institutions, but to let God develop their talent in a way that their character becomes so exceptional that the liberals they work with cannot avoid their influence. At the same time, they must be completely prepared to withstand the temptations of the world. As mentioned above, Christian churches, colleges, internships, and schools will have to create programs directed at training and supporting the warriors who will be intersecting the kingdom of this world. They will be specialized cultural missionaries.

The next section is a warning to those called into the high places of society. We cannot see ourselves as part of the elite. Once Christian believers see themselves as better than others, those Christians fall into the elitist trap.

Intelligentsia Trap

One of the most powerful traps Culture Warriors face is when they move into influential careers with the promise of becoming important, superior, and powerful. The ego, or *self*, desires all those worldly accomplishments. Most people want to have a position above the common person, or the masses. That is why God often chooses the weaker and younger as his instruments, such as Gideon or David. If they begin to take credit for their accomplishments, God can and will remind them of where they came from and who brought them their success. Pride and arrogance are the greatest temptations and means for failure for a future Culture Warrior.

God broke his model for choosing disciples when he chose Paul. Paul was a classic example of an elitist before his conversion. He was a Pharisee of Pharisees, studying under the greatly respected Jewish rabbi Gamaliel. Paul said, "For you have heard of my former conduct in Judaism, how I persecuted the church of God beyond measure and *tried* to destroy it. And I advanced in Judaism beyond many of my contemporaries in my own nation, being more exceedingly zealous for the traditions of my fathers" (Gal. 1:13, 14). As a rabbi, he saw Christians as lowly, dangerous rabble. They were fishermen, tax collectors, women, and other lower-class people. He believed they were uneducated and unintelligent and therefore easily deceived by a charismatic leader like Jesus. He placed great importance upon his superior intelligence and behavior. He followed the religious laws and looked down on the common people and non-Jews. He was especially prejudiced against the Gentiles as were all religious Jews of the time. The Gentiles lacked guidance from the Law and the prophets and therefore acted immorally, especially in sexual behavior.

God broke through to Paul by a dramatic intervention in his life on the road to Damascus. Without that event, Paul would have remained an elitist. The contrast between his elite status and apostle status is clear. As an elitist, he expected everyone to pay him great respect and deference for his superiority. He exercised power without mercy and self-righteously felt justified to kill innocent men and women. Once he was converted, Paul learned what it really meant to be a servant. He worked as a tentmaker to keep from asking for support from churches, even though he had every right to ask for it. He suffered more persecution and violence than any other apostle. He didn't consider where he lived, how he was treated, if he possessed anything of value, or whether anyone respected him. He was broken before God, only concerned with pleasing Him and becoming like Jesus. He was stripped of pride, feelings of superiority, and arrogance. He understood that his intellect meant nothing if God didn't first transform it into godly wisdom. He is the example for our specialized Culture Warriors.

Of course, Jesus was naturally and supernaturally superior in intelligence to the Pharisees, political leaders, and scholars of the time, but he didn't separate himself from the people. He identified with them and valued their minds and talents. He was one of them at the same time He was their leader. Being a leader didn't remove him from valuing and respecting less intelligent and talented people. They were equal in value because Christ values all human life, having created humans in His image and likeness and having become one of them. He spoke of this humble attitude in the Beatitudes about the poor in spirit and the meek. For elitists, this is incomprehensible. They disrespect the masses and feel a sense of entitlement and superiority because of their intelligence and other talents.

Superiority and pride are a great temptation for anyone who attends a prestigious university. The elitist club is open to anyone from any class who has elevated intelligence. Also required is a rejection of a simple faith in God. An elitist cannot be simple. Simplicity and faith are seen as naive. The elites think they know the truth about society and how it works. They see themselves as its compassionate, tolerant caretakers and rulers, and they believe they are entitled to live their lives without the moral and ethical values of the Judeo-Christian traditional society. They tell themselves the masses cannot truly rule or take care of themselves. They think common people are easily manipulated by religion to judge those who act immorally. Liberal, progressive elites want the freedom to pursue whatever behavior they feel like pursuing. They linger in the 1960s idea of "If it feels good, do it."

The present elites that have revolutionized American values and principles are not the elites of the past. The elites of the past were more in agreement with the values of the masses as established by Christian influence.

The Power Elite by C. Wright Mills is a classic study. During the period that he wrote this book—the 1950s—the elite consisted of the military, corporations, and government. They exercised the most power in society. They were not liberal but conservative in their values although still, if possessing too much power, a threat to a free society. For centuries the influential elites had been conservative, and their standards were conservative; they were identified as the aristocrats of society. However, since the twentieth century the most influential elites have thrown out the traditional values and replaced them with relative morality. It's this group who provide the most temptation for the Culture Warriors. The liberal elites don't want to lose the hold they have on the culture, and they are looking for new elites who will be enticed by the pride and power to become part of the intelligentsia.

Culture Warriors have to avoid the temptations that will be presented by the elite group that greatly impacts our culture. It will take an excellent spirit to avoid putting oneself above the majority of people. The ego is inflated and access to power and influence is a heady pleasure.

Bernard Goldberg, in his book *100 People Who Are Screwing Up America*, described the kind of superior attitudes the elites feel toward Middle America:

> Yes, there is real resentment, indeed. Middle Americans resent the smug condescension the elites routinely dish out from their cocoons in Manhattan and Hollywood. They resent the authors and journalists who call them "ignorant" because they can't see things the way the elites do. They resent the elites snickering at them because they like to bowl and eat at Red Lobster. They resent the notion that because they go to church every week and take the Bible seriously that there's something creepy about them, and that because they fly the American flag on the fourth of July they're simple-minded and hayseeds."[1]

Personal Experience

When attending U of C in Santa Barbara, I was very intent upon doing well in my classes. In high school I was more interested in student activities; I was sophomore class president, a cheerleader in my junior year, and ASB president in my senior year. I wanted to serve my school and didn't concentrate on my grades. There-fore, when I started college, I knew I would have to work hard to establish better study habits if I wanted to do well. I didn't pledge in a sorority and spent hours in the library. Because I began to excel in my academics (in most of my classes), some of the intellectu-als began to approach me. They befriended me for a time. We had intellectual discussions, and they measured me to see if I would fit into their social status. As time went on and I expressed my strong belief in God and Jesus—they withdrew. I didn't meet their criteria to enter elite circles.

It was the time in which the civil rights movement and free speech movement at Berkeley were active. I considered attending Berkeley to get into that movement, but the Lord kept me from going down that path. Also, I had planned to become a lawyer and go into politics. Again the Lord clearly revealed to me that if I went down that path I would be morally corrupted. He knew that lib-eralism was on the rise, and that I would be sucked into the liberal values that would have violated my conscience and undermined my faith. He spoke to me about my vulnerability during a class on business ethics. I could see from what I learned in that class that the temptations in business, politics, and other high places were beyond my moral foundation at that time. I thank God that He made it very clear to me in my senior year of college to choose a different path.

Personal Experience

Another experience of mine that might be helpful to others is the time I ran for Congress in 2002. I was the Republican candidate for Congress in a San Jose district. I was a member of the local cen-tral committee. The role of the central committee is to help can-didates get elected. In Santa Clara County, the Republican Party was divided into two divergent branches, the conservatives and the liberals (although they call themselves moderates). Rush Limbaugh calls them *country club* Republicans and conservatives call them RINOS—Republicans in Name Only. The liberals were socially liberal while economically conservative, and the conservatives were economically *and* socially conservative.

The goal was supposed to be to work together to get Republicans elected, but the liberal Republicans identified more with the Democratic Central Committee than the conservative Republicans on their own central committee. Those who controlled the Democratic Central Committee were liberal elites. They supported abortion and homosexual marriage as well as redistribution of wealth through bigger government and higher taxes. Although the liberal Republicans didn't agree with the Democrats' views on taxes or the size of government, they felt more unity with the Democrats because of their attitudes toward social issues and their feelings of superiority to conservatives in the party. They saw conservatives as inferior intellectually and ignorant.

One of my supporters went onto the Democratic Central Committee's Web site and found the minutes to one of their meetings. In the minutes, they explained how they had been in contact with liberal Republicans and were joining with them to keep me from getting elected. They also stated they could not let someone with my ideas win a Republican primary in the future.

It was not surprising but it was disappointing. In those kinds of frustrating situations, Culture Warriors have to trust God to show them how to overcome internal resistance. I didn't win the election, but I am certain God had a broader purpose for my running for office. Nothing is lost in God's kingdom; every act in His will produces fruit.

Everything takes time and many seeds are planted and grow that we don't see. We have to live in persevering faith to allow God to make a way for us to intersect with the kingdom of this world. God's warriors will move toward accomplishing His goal with every step of obedience. God's plan is to return America to its foundational principles and to restore the Judeo-Christian fabric of American society. It will happen as long as modern warriors answer God's call, just as the Puritan warriors obeyed God's call to leave England and sacrifice their lives to fulfill God's plan for the kingdom of God.

Job-Related Small Groups

For years churches have provided small-group meetings with Bible study guides. Lessons have related to general themes in Scripture or an expository approach. At this time of warfare, Culture Warriors would benefit more by having groups that relate Scripture to workplace issues. Many decisions at work have moral consequences and complications. In addition, people could come and share their struggles and victories and ask for prayer and guidance. Some people spend more time at work than at home. Their concerns at work would provide in-depth and intellectually challenging topics for discussion and biblical research. They would produce the opportunities to apply spiritual principles and moral laws to workplace circumstances. These small groups would be a source of prayer for each member and for their workplace.

Sometimes workplace problems become a topic for a small group, but it's a greatly neglected area. It consumes so many people's lives, and they find very few places to explore all the struggles they face with managers, fellow employees, customers, and policies. It would not take much to focus a small group around workplace issues and open the door for prayer to reestablish Christian principles into people's jobs. All the moral issues faced in life appear in the workplace. It could also provide a means to develop plans on how to influence that particular workplace for Christ and His principles.

Another kind of small group could be formed from Christians at the worksite that are from different churches. They could meet outside the workplace, such as for lunch once a week. They could study the Bible, discuss problems, and pray for the business and relationships that might be causing problems. Through prayer, they could orchestrate God's plan for various situations and projects, and for evangelism. This can be a very effective way to bring Christ into the workplace and His principles back into the culture.

Prayer and fasting for the nation is another important role for career-focused groups. The importance of being God's warriors is seen in 2 Chronicles 7:14 (NIV): "If my people, which are called by my name, shall humble themselves, and pray, and seek my face, and turn from their wicked ways; then will I hear from heaven, and will forgive their sin, and will heal their land."

This Scripture has been the theme for Christians concerned with our culture since the 1970s. And in Daniel 9 we see a prayer that should become our model and inspiration:

> As *it is* written in the Law of Moses, all this disaster has come upon us; yet we have not made our prayer before the LORD our God, that we might turn from our iniquities and understand Your truth. Therefore the LORD has kept the disaster in mind, and brought it upon us; for the LORD our God *is* righteous in all the works which He does, though we have not obeyed His voice. And now, O Lord our God, who brought Your people out of the land of Egypt with a mighty hand, and made Yourself a name, as *it is* this day—we have sinned, we have done wickedly!
>
> O Lord, according to all Your righteousness, I pray, let Your anger and Your fury be turned away from Your city Jerusalem, Your holy mountain; because for our sins, and for the iniquities of our fathers, Jerusalem and Your people *are* a reproach to all *those* around us.
>
> Now therefore, our God, hear the prayer of Your servant, and his supplications, and for the Lord's sake cause Your face to shine on Your sanctuary, which is desolate. O my God, incline Your ear and hear; open Your eyes and see our desolations, and the city which is called by Your name; for we do not present our supplications before You because of our righteous deeds, but because of Your great mercies. O Lord, hear! O Lord, forgive! O Lord, listen and act! Do not delay for Your own sake, my God, for Your city and Your people are called by Your name. (Dan. 9:13–19)

We are in the same state as a nation as Israel was at that time of Daniel's prayer. Intercessory prayer is the force to break Satan's hold on the culture. In intercessory prayer we can practice our two roles: Christ in us and us being in Christ. With *Christ in us*, we can hear His instructions, reassurance, and direction. The Holy Spirit can reveal the Lord's plan, step by step, and give us the peace and confirmation we are in His will. However, when we are *in Christ*, we are able to rule with him "far above all principality and power and might and dominion" (Eph. 1:21). In Christ, we can force the *Enemy* and his henchmen to their knees. We can conquer them and chain them back in Hell.

Previous Efforts

Christians have not been passive during the Culture War. There have been valiant and powerful efforts to win the war. However, in spite of many efforts, we appear to be losing the Culture War. We have made progress and then suffered reversals. At times, it has been disheartening. The next section describes some of these heroic efforts of earlier Culture Warriors.

Christian and Traditional Strategies

Some Christian and traditionalist messengers, such as Jerry Falwell, Pat Robertson, Beverly LaHaye, and Bill O'Reilly, have sounded the alarm to warn the American public about Culture War issues. Different strategies for winning this war have been tried, but none of them has provided true success. The reason for our failures or partial successes in previous efforts is the result of our failure to understand the strategy of the Enemy and, therefore, concentrate our efforts most efficiently and effectively. We have not understood where "the accursed" things are hidden among us and how we can remove them.

Our past battle plans concentrated upon revealing and explaining that there was a war on our culture—more of a wake-up call. We expected Christians and our more traditional citizens to react with outrage and action. We expected them to respond by resisting its ungodly principles and recommitting to Judeo-Christian ones. The exposure strategy has had only partial success. The power of sin and the powerful brainwashing of the media have prevented Christian strategies from succeeding. Americans, Christians included, find it too difficult to think clearly and support godly laws and godly leaders. Secular progressives exert great pressure on the minds and emotions of Americans through control of the media and schools, confusing and diluting their courage and determination to do what is right.

The other line of attack against socialists has been to focus upon electing leaders who understand we are in a Culture War and will fight for righteous laws. This strategy also has had only partial success because laws cannot change the thinking or feelings of citizens. Plus, the Left has been successful in undermining the effectiveness of politicians, using strategies of ridicule, mockery, and personal attacks. Our goal is to actually restore Judeo-Christian principles by returning to the institutions the Left used to revolutionize our society. The information above lays out what has to be done to prepare and send Christian warriors back into the culture. The next chapter will provide more information about the socialist plan, methods, and tactics. We will not be effective and powerful in institutions unless we learn how to disarm the weapons of our socialist, progressive, secular opponents. Chapter eight will explain Saul Alinsky liberal tactics and show how to disarm and neutralize them.

Tactical Training for Culture Warriors

Psalm 83
A Song. A Psalm of Asaph.
Do not keep silent, O God!
Do not hold Your peace,
And do not be still, O God!
For behold, Your enemies make a tumult;
And those who hate You have lifted up their head.
They have taken crafty counsel against Your people,
And consulted together against Your sheltered ones.
They have said, "Come, and let us cut them off from *being* a nation,
That the name of Israel may be remembered no more."
For they have consulted together with one consent;
They form a confederacy against You:

Who said, "Let us take for ourselves
The pastures of God for a possession."

Personal Experience

Astudent in my class at the University of Phoenix manifested the craftiness and hatred expressed in the passage above. Her attitude and actions gave me a great insight into the inner satisfaction and sense of power that drives those in our culture who want to rule it. She supported euthanasia, doctor-assisted suicide, and abortion, based upon the argument that quality of life surpassed the value of life when making decisions about life and death. She thought you should end the life of the unborn who had some defect, concluding they would rather not exist than have a limited quality of life. She felt qualified to make that decision for the unborn and for other members of society who were no longer able to contribute or enjoy life as she felt was right.

When she wrote her ideas in essays, I could feel her satisfaction at being able to replace God in making life-and-death decisions. She even strutted around the classroom, defying anyone to disagree with her.

She was motivated by a feeling of powerlessness. She competed with other class members to prove she was the best and brightest, and demanded a good grade. She could not work with a team because she wanted to produce all the team assignments without interference from her teammates. She punished anyone who crossed her will. To her, she had won the power struggle and was superior to those she held captive by her demand to speak her ideas without anyone opposing them. She was in charge and if you resisted her, she would take revenge by complaining and charging others had a personal grudge.

I identified her behavior with that of many of the people in poverty and deprivation that Saul Alinsky organized to gain their rights. Not that there were not injustices. The Have-nots of society were for centuries ignored and abused. Many economic injustices increased during the Industrial Revolution. Alinsky worked tirelessly to help the poorest overcome those economic injustices. Many times he succeeded in righting many wrongs. His mistake was creating his own utilitarian ethical system. As he explained, "THAT

PERENNIAL QUESTION, 'Does the end justify the means?' is meaningless as it stands; the real and only question regarding the ethics of means and ends is, and always has been, 'Does this *particular* end justify this *particular* means?'"[1] With this kind of immoral thinking, he corrupted the Have-nots in the process of trying to help them. It was the manipulation and methods Alinsky used that soured his accomplishments. He played on the emotions of Have-nots to gain their support and created in them a victim mentality. He didn't train them to become contributing members of society but to take from others what he told them belonged to them. Increasing self-pity, he drove them to anger and to seek revenge.

I will not explain all of Alinsky's goals and how he accomplished them. Alinsky developed highly insidious tactics to achieve his goals for the Have-nots. He was a community organizer, and he trained community organizers. He followed Marxist ideas while adding his own experiences to his approach and was an admitted socialist. Our concern in this book is his tactics rather than studying individual cases of his successes. As mentioned earlier, President Obama learned many of his techniques and ideas from disciples of Alinsky in Chicago. Knowledge of Alinsky's tactics can help us understand the methods used by the far Left presently in many of the arenas of politics and other Left-controlled institutions.

Alinsky painted the American bourgeois culture as unjust and the cause of poverty. It made the Have-nots feel they deserved better jobs and treatment without having to earn them, using threats to gain their objectives. He also made them feel morally superior to the Haves in society. Such ideas led to a sense of power in making demands on corporations and society. They sought to make up their own rules out of a sense of revenge and superiority, leading to unrealistic expectations.

These ideas resulted in a god-complex, which is often seen in the Have-nots who are influenced by the liberal elite. Both the elite and the Have-nots have a god-complex. As mentioned in the Scripture above, Alinsky's method challenged God and wanted to cut off His nation from its roots. They "consulted" together to find a way to remove the objective truths and Judeo-Christian principles from our society. Then they could determine right and wrong and justice and injustice. They could eliminate any traditions that stood in the way of their desires. They were much like the masses in the French Revolution, who thought they could rule righteously without having any principles to guide them except revenge and self-gratification. Of course, they ended their reign of terror in anarchy and the need for Napoleon to restore order.

Socialist Confederacy

The scriptural passage above speaks of the very action and method of those anti-God and anti-Christian opponents of the twentieth century. It can be applied to America: "They have taken crafty counsel against Your people, and consulted together against Your sheltered ones" (v. 3). In other words, God's adversaries joined together to make a plan against God's people. It has happened throughout the world, and America has, in spite of its moral flaws, resisted for many years. However, our opponents' goals are almost accomplished. Their goal was to cut America off from being God's chosen nation. The same enemy cut off Israel many centuries ago and only in the last days will they be restored. America is also a chosen nation, and the Enemy is again trying to cut us off as he did Israel. However, that is not God's plan or intention. His gifts and callings are without repentance, and no prophecy predicts our downfall. We have a covenant which will remain until the "fullness of the Gentiles" is complete and Israel is grafted back into the Vine.

The restoration of America will not happen without a well-thought-out plan, as mentioned in the last chapter, and we must be realistic that this is a long-range plan. It took socialists more than fifty years to successfully achieve their revolution. We must be patient in our counterrevolution. The Holy Spirit, the strategist for our plan, may work more quickly, but we must not put a timeline on our commitment or the commitment of future generations.

We will not copy the strategy of our opponents, but we will defuse and disarm it. They use manipulation, browbeating, and deception to win their battles. We have a higher purpose and a higher calling. We will begin with obedience to reenter the culture. Once we begin, God will reveal His innocent but shrewd tactics, far superior to our adversaries.' We will disarm our adversaries. However, we will not know everything we are to do until we begin to do it. We only know we must prepare and become disciples for this age. God will train and prepare us and when we put what we learn into practice, God will amaze us with the gifts and talents He provides beyond anything we could imagine or anticipate.

How to Disarm Socialist Weapons

> Behold, I send you out as sheep in the midst of wolves. Therefore be wise as serpents and harmless as doves. But beware of men, for they will deliver you up to councils and scourge you in their synagogues. You will be brought before governors and kings for My sake, as a testimony to them and to the Gentiles. But when they deliver you up, do not worry about how or what you should speak. For it will be given to you in that hour what you should speak; for it is not you who speak, but the Spirit of your Father who speaks in you. (Matt. 10:16–20)

Remember, as Culture Warriors, you are going into battle as sheep among wolves. You are sheep in that you are to remain innocent of bitterness and revenge. You cannot use dishonest or evil tactics to win your battles. The end never justifies the means. However, you are shrewd sheep that can win battles without losing your innocence.

Two ideas stand out as instructions from this biblical quotation: First, we are to be "wise as serpents and harmless as doves." Some translations use the word *shrewd*, which I think applies in the situation facing Culture Warriors. Christians can sometimes be too naive and soft when facing an enemy, especially one that has been well trained to defeat us. We must be shrewd in a godly manner. In other words, we can know our opponents' strategy and find ways to make it ineffective. We can go into battle with a strategy to disarm the weapons of our foes.

Jesus goes on to say, "But when they deliver you up, don't worry about how or what you should speak. For it will be given to you in that hour what you should speak; for it is not you who speak, but the Spirit of your Father who speaks in you." The Holy Spirit will guide us to plan a strategy, and He will also be there to put His words in our mouths when we are uncertain what to say. We have a Counselor and a Truth-speaker who can undo the worldly wisdom of the most intelligent and mocking opponents. Do not be afraid or resistant to going into battles; embrace the battles with vigor and trust God to make you victorious.

Jesus used certain methods to answer his critics. He often called them hypocrites and directly refuted their false accusations. This technique can work under certain circumstances when there are no television cameras. Nowadays those trying to catch a warrior in a mistake or misstep use our anger to make us look mean-spirited and cruel. This age doesn't allow as much direct response with righteous anger. Jesus also used parables to disarm His enemies, and we can, if so gifted, be folksy, using a story to get across our points. Only some people have this talent, but it's a good one to develop. I will give an example of President Reagan's approach later, and he had that ability.

As mentioned in chapter one, to be victorious, Culture Warriors will have to acquire weapons to disarm the tactics of their opponents. Sending warriors into battle requires extensive training and preparation. They have to attend warrior boot camp to become skilled soldiers.

We will not adopt the strategy or tactics of our opponents. We will not deceive and manipulate the public to achieve our end. Socialists have developed vicious and disparaging techniques that ignore the human dignity of their targets. They see the opposition as evil and undeserving of mercy or compassion—the end justifies the means. They have objectified the opposition, so their hearts will not be touched by the damage and disruption they impose on their victims. I remember Ross Perot's surprise when he created the Reform Party for the 1992 presidential election and became its presidential candidate. After years of business dealings, he was confronted with a scheme that shocked him. He said he was threatened with some kind of disruption of his daughter's wedding. He never made clear what was threatened, but whatever it was, it shocked and alarmed him. His temporary withdrawal from the presidential race was all it took for his enemies to say he was a kook and paranoid. The subsequent ridicule ended his chance to win. The strategy worked. (I don't know which party used the techniques. There are times some Republicans have adopted some of the same methods, but still it's primarily liberal Democrats who use them.)

In this chapter, we are focusing on those tactics developed by Saul Alinsky because they have been very successful for the last forty years. They are the tactics that have most undermined Christians and conservatives who have been fighting in the Culture War. They are not applied only in political situations but also in the workplace and at community meetings. Much too often, these devices have been successful and turned our efforts into a tool for our own self-destruction. We will begin with three of Alinsky's tactics that have been most successful:

Alinsky's Rule Number Five

Rule number five was already mentioned in chapter one: It's ridicule. *"Ridicule is man's most potent weapon,"* wrote Alinsky. "It's almost impossible to counterattack ridicule."[2] Socialists find ways to laugh at their enemies so they can dismiss them intellectually. This tactic was constantly used on former President George W. Bush. Once the news media found his Achilles heel in his speaking errors, they could point to him as intellectually diminished and incapable of making difficult decisions. The constant drip of condescension wore into the consciousness of the public, robbing Bush of their respect and support. Since he would not fight back using the same techniques, he could not overcome the battering by the press and far-left Democrats.

Recently there was a campaign to associate the Republican Party with Rush Limbaugh. Limbaugh is a controversial and extremely outspoken radio personality. It was a form of ridicule to identify the

Republican Party with him. Since many people see Limbaugh as an extremist and a fanatic, the Left hoped to marginalize the Republican Party the same way they did Bush.

In this case, Bill O'Reilly from Fox News mentioned the tactic to associate Limbaugh with the Republicans as one of Alinksy's rules. O'Reilly had on a guest he asked if that was the technique the Left was using. The guest evaded answering the question, but in the end, the exposure put a stop to the tactic. It was a great help that O'Reilly was not under personal attack himself, so he could expose the method.

Alinsky gave an example of how he used ridicule against a W. Allen Wallis. He was in a conflict with him over the demands of a black organization. Wallis was the president of the University of Rochester and later a director of Eastman Kodak. The warfare between him and Alinsky ended when Alinsky responded to a questioner, "'Wallis?' I replied. 'Which one are you talking about—Wallace of Alabama, or Wallis of Rochester—but I guess there isn't any difference, so what was your question?'" Alinsky went on to describe Wallis's reaction: "This reply (1) introduced an element of ridicule and (2) it ended any further attacks from the president of the University of Rochester, who began to suspect that he was going to be shafted with razors, and that an encounter with me or with my associates was not going to be an academic dialogue."[3]

Alinsky's Rule Number Thirteen

"Pick the target, freeze it, personalize it, and polarize it."[4] The target is "singled out and frozen" by naming an individual, not a board or group, as the one responsible for some failed policy or apparent injustice. "In other words, there must be a face associated with the people's discontent."[5]

The "freezing" and "personalizing" of former President George W. Bush also reveals the great success of this tactic. First he was intellectually humiliated and then morally crushed. Bush became the personification of evil by the end of his term. By constant criticism, especially by the liberal news media, the Iraq

War became the albatross around Bush's neck. The public was fed only the negative aspects of the war, finally stripping Bush of any moral standing. The plan was to polarize the issues so Bush was seen as 100 percent evil. Alinsky further explained, "One acts decisively only in the conviction that all the angels are on one side and all the devils on the other."[6] The news media and the Left succeeded in putting all the devils on Bush's side. Even since he left office, they have continued to throw aspersions upon him and his decisions.

Another person to whom this tactic has been applied is Sarah Palin. She stepped down as governor of Alaska because of ongoing lawsuits, trying to smear her as "evil" and unethical. It was costing Alaska and her family thousands of dollars to fight those frivolous lawsuits. The strategy to crush her continued after the presidential election because the Left wanted to knock her out of any possibility to run for president in 2012 since she had charisma and power as a politician and woman.

Alinsky's Rule Four

"Make the enemy live up to their own book of rules. You can kill them with this, for they can no more obey their own rules than the Christian church can live up to Christianity."[7] This rule was used against Carrie Prejean, as mentioned above. Sarah Palin also had to fight the implications that her daughter's pregnancy outside of marriage was an example of the failure of Palin's ability as a mother to live up to her Christian values.

Christians and conservatives are often vulnerable to the "book of rules" attack since very few Christians have avoided doing something at some point in their life that could be later used against them. Also, sadly, many Christians become involved in wrongdoing after they have committed their lives to the Lord. Politicians and other well-known Christians are often exposed in sinful circumstances, bringing shame on the reputation of all Christians as well as God's good name. For this reason, Culture Warriors need the Christian boot camp and follow-up support groups mentioned in chapter seven. We cannot continue to be such poor representatives of our Lord and Savior.

Interestingly, the liberals take rule four very personally. There is a great competition in their minds between secular progressives and Christians. Since they violate many of the moral laws, such as sex before marriage, abortion, and adultery, they strongly feel the need to show how much more righteous they are than Christians. Sometimes it becomes a personal vendetta, needing to prove to their own consciences that they are better than God's children.

Recommendations

The following are recommendations on how to handle various attacks. We are not trying to attack back or ever use the Left's tactics; however, we need to know how to disarm their weapons, which will have an impact on other people who see the interaction. These tactics can apply to a private job situation involving other employees and managers, or a public situation involving media-focused attacks. Some of the following defensive weapons have to be adjusted for your own situations. They are more of a guide to the tone and attitude rather than an exact formula. I have found that the Holy Spirit is the best guide in spelling out what to say and do.

In Response to the Three Rules

How do you defuse the three rules above and their complements? It's difficult to try to give instructions to fit every situation. Instead, I will present a list of what not to do and the kind of attitude and words to use that weaken or make ineffective methods of one's opponents. The goal of all three strategies is to cause the one attacked to react. You should react but the reaction has to be well planned.

Most important is to realize that God through His Holy Spirit plans to lead you step by step through a strategy to win. Pray before each decision. When you are under attack, I recommend you meet with others for prayer as often as necessary to receive God's instructions. As you seek Him and read the Word and become quiet, you will be able to hear the Spirit in your spirit and soul. Join with others to receive direction.

Response to Ridicule

If the ridicule is not being done in front of millions or on local news but is at work in some limited circumstance, then try to resolve the problem personally. When being ridiculed by a number of people, approach the leader of those doing the mocking and talk to that person alone. Do not try to confront or talk to a group of your opponents. Many of them are being manipulated and don't understand it's all a strategy. When you talk to your opponent, don't attack or challenge. If possible, catch that person on the run, after a meeting or after work, rather than setting up a formal meeting. Speak in a humble, nonthreatening manner, such as:

"I don't understand why . . ."

"You may not realize what you are doing . . ."

"I'm sure you don't mean to be rude or insulting, but . . ."

"I was disappointed that . . ."

I had an opportunity to practice this strategy when I was elected to a school board in San Jose in 1998. None of the school board members knew me before I won. They may have greeted me and that was all. I had moved to San Jose from Palo Alto two years earlier, so no one really knew my political views. They just knew I was a friend of a dedicated community servant and volunteer. He had founded a neighborhood group some twenty-five years earlier and had done a great service to the Berryessa area in San Jose. His name is Bill Hughes.

Bill was not only a community volunteer but also a conservative Republican. Once I was seen with Bill, I was labeled a conservative. When I joined the school board, the members, who were all liberals, immediately shunned me and treated me rudely. I was the enemy and, being a conservative, they felt I must be heartless. They were sure I ran for school board not because I cared about the children in the district, but had run under false pretenses. They thought my main goal was to push my conservative, religious agenda onto the district. However, my first goal was to be a school board member, taking each issue individually in making my decisions. They had misjudged my motives.

Their treatment was a lesson in ridicule. I remember one time walking with other members to our meeting and cracking a joke about something personal—a self-reference joke—and no one laughed. They all ignored me as if I hadn't spoken. Also, when I would mention something about my life in which I helped children, being a foster mom or helping inner-city kids, again they would not respond. It was as if I wasn't even there. They could not believe I cared about children or that I had genuine feelings of compassion. I was an impersonal monster to them. During the meetings, some of them would roll their eyes when I spoke. If I tried to make a light comment, they would frown. They set a tone and mood to make it impossible for me to speak fluently. I always felt a pressure to "shut up." They made me feel as if I were stupid, and they tried to make the audience feel the same way.

Their main goal was to make me angry so I would act out and look outrageous to the public. They had treated a previous member the same way. She became angry and began to write and speak out against the board. In response, antagonistic board members passed out to the community hit pieces, editorials, and flyers exposing her private life. As she showed more anger, she looked increasingly unstable to the voters and, therefore, lost the next election. Their strategy to use ridicule to trigger anger worked against her. She was the victim, but her reactions made the other board members look like the victims.

I was aware of these games and avoided them. One of the members, the president, was the ringleader. One evening after the board meeting I walked out to her car with her. I said something like: "I know you must not mean to be rude to me or are unaware you are being rude, but I heard that some of the people attending the meetings are wondering, 'Why are they so mean to Mrs. Hermann?' It's causing concern to the public. I know you don't want people to think we are not a united school board. Maybe you could watch what you say and do in the future, so the public won't get the wrong idea?"

When I was done, she appeared to be crying. The way I presented my case didn't give her any means to respond critically. Anyway, she didn't say anything. She just got into her car and drove away. From then on, I was never treated as rudely again. The other board members were more polite and attentive. Once the two most prejudiced members of the board retired, our school board, according to a board consultant, became one of the most united boards she had ever advised. The tactic of approaching the ringleader worked.

Response to Freezing or Personalizing the Target and Using a Person's Rules against Them

First, never respond to offenses out of anger publicly—to others on the job or to the public—even if you are furious. Getting us to respond with anger is a strategy of the Left. It's part of Alinsky's instructions when he tries to polarize and demonize his opponent. He added three instructions to the tactic: (1) "The real action is in the enemy's reaction." (2) "The enemy properly goaded and guided in his reaction will be your major strength." (3) "Tactics, like organizations, like life, require that you move with the action."[8] Their goal is for us to show anger and appear to be the "bad guy," making them the victims. Then people feel sorry for them, not us.

If you noticed, President Bush didn't fight back against his opponents. He tried to explain his positions and decisions, but he never responded with anger. If he had responded with anger, he would have been hated even more. However, his response didn't work that well because so much of the news media constantly attacked him, and he did invite attacks once he chose to go into Iraq for more reasons than he initially stated. Because of the need for national security, he could not give all the information the public needed to defend his position. I think he decided that his Iraq strategy needed to be followed no matter the cost to him personally, his party, or his administration. History will vindicate or condemn his decision.

In order to avoid being trapped by the two tactics above, we have to protect ourselves from false accusations. In order to defend ourselves, we must be totally prepared to live an exemplary life. In that case, any accusations will not be true. When the accusations are false, we can confront the lies more directly. However, again, don't show much anger and be prepared with complete documentation, witnesses if necessary, and records. Speak as I mentioned above. Something like: "I don't understand how someone could falsely accuse me. They could have asked me privately before making it public. I'm sure they didn't do it to harm me; they must have been misled by others." This is just an example of the spirit of our response. Find out all the facts that support our case and decision. Ask God for insight into what is the strategy of our opponents. Hopefully, it can be done privately.

Personal Experience

When I was on the school board, some of the members leaked information about a superintendent's search. Leaking information about certain school board business is a violation of the Brown Act in California. The superintendent candidate who was involved discovered the leak and told me about it. I called and asked our lawyers if the leak was a violation of the Brown Act because I wanted to stop any more leaks. The lawyers called the school board together in a private meeting. I was surprised when the lawyers and other school board members came to the meeting ready to charge me with violating the Brown Act. They attacked me in order to protect their illegal activities and also in hopes they could find a reason to seek to recall me.

I was surprised at first, but I had come prepared. I had documented all my conversations with each person involved. I had information from the candidate for superintendent that proved two of the board members had been leaking information. We argued for at least forty-five minutes, but finally, they were disarmed. They had no proof I violated the law. I proved *they* had violated the Brown Act.

We separated with them wondering if I was going to charge them with the violation. I could have filed a complaint with the civil grand jury. I didn't expose them; rather I insisted we all be more careful in the future. I didn't want to remove them; I just wanted to stop them from doing it again and hopefully, through showing mercy, find a way we could work together.

Further Recommendations

If you are in the public eye, you must define yourself—or the media will define you. It's much more difficult to fight the news media and liberal elites whose television programs are totally involved in mockery, such as *The Daily Show* and *Saturday Night Live*. Yes, you do usually need to go on them to show your good sense of humor; however, that is not all you can do.

Sarah Palin reacted in anger to the belittling of the press. Their goal was to define her to the public as unprepared and lacking the knowledge to be vice president. Her goal was to defy their definition. By responding with anger, she entered their trap. She took some missteps that were difficult to undo. Her best response would have followed President Reagan's method.

Ronald Reagan was the master of defining himself and resisting the presses' efforts to label him. His greatest weapon was self-deprecating humor. By using himself as the butt of jokes, he was able to avoid appearing arrogant or pompous. People are willing to forgive a humble person, but they will judge an arrogant one or someone who appears arrogant. Reagan was one of "the people." He didn't separate himself or think he was smarter or better than regular people. Suzanne Adelson wrote an online article about a writer, Doug Gamble, who gave Reagan many of his self-deprecating jokes. She wrote, "Remember how Reagan defused questions about his old age? 'I think that remark accusing me of having amnesia was uncalled for,' the President would tell adoring audiences and, 'I just wish I could remember who said it.'"[9]

Let's apply his principle to Sarah Palin. When Katie Couric put her on the spot as to what news magazines she read, if she really didn't have time to keep up with all the national news, she could have joked about fitting in reading national news magazines between reading about Alaska's state problems and reading Dr. Seuss to Piper and soon to Trig. Further she could have humbly and jokingly described how all working mothers have to have gigantic abilities to multitask. Then she could have related the struggle to Katie Couric's own efforts to multitask. Finally, Palin could have related her abilities to adapt to new challenges as do all working mothers in the United States. This scenario would have worked to her advantage and allowed her to be honest if she didn't have much time to read national news magazines.

It's surprising that George W. Bush was not able to use Reagan's method to confound the liberal press. He had some of the same speechwriters. In addition, he was a very sociable and likeable guy. He was popular and personable in college. Part of his problem was his inability to communicate freely and smoothly in front of large numbers of people. He was not relaxed or comfortable before television audiences. His self-deprecation did help him seem more regular to the public, but without a more comfortable style, he could not succeed in resisting the labels as Reagan did.

More Alinsky

Before moving on, we need to review a few other Alinsky rules: He said to keep a constant pressure on the opposition by using a variety of tactics and actions and to go outside the experience of the enemy.[10] For example, when I was ambushed by the district lawyers and school board members, it was an effort to make me go outside my experience. However, I had some past experience in having to defend myself, so I was prepared. If they had tried to attack me publicly, it would have been more difficult. I had never had to defend myself to the public. If they had attacked me publicly about some other issue, not with a Brown Act violation because that could not go public, I would have used my column in a small local paper and my television show on the community channel to describe how they must be confused or uninformed to have attacked me. I would have resisted showing anger and, instead, talked about how they had not done their homework in trying to accuse me of something I didn't do. I would have had an advantage because I had some resources to reach the public.

Again, I reiterate, never show anger when you are on the defense. You can show anger when on the offense. Your adversary may have done something wrong that needs to be exposed if personal intervention cannot resolve it. Then, you can show righteous anger if the action deserves it. The public accepts righteous anger when it's an offensive, not a defensive, strategy. For example, President Kennedy publicly showed anger toward the steel industry when he had made an agreement that the unions would not ask for increased wages if the steel companies would not raise prices. When steel raised its prices, Kennedy spoke out strongly against them and it worked. His anger was real and the public agreed.

Another example would be former Vice President Cheney's response to the Obama administration's criticism of the Bush homeland security policies. In this case, anger didn't turn the public away from him because Cheney had no plan to seek public office. His defense came out of a concern not only to defend his administration's previous policies but also out of an unselfish desire to keep Americans safe. He feared that the Obama administration would jeopardize Americans' safety in its efforts to heap scorn on Republicans.

Trained Alinsky Followers

You will not find persecution on every job. There are more trained liberals in some areas of the country than others. Also, some careers draw more attacks, such as the news media, politics, entertainment, education, and the courts. If you decide to be a journalist, you will find prejudice against conservatives from most of your university professors and from many publishers and/or editors. If you go into the movie industry, you will be pressured to adopt liberal causes. In politics, of course, in a liberal area like the Bay Area, there will be some Alinsky-trained disciples in most political offices. Some disciples may not even know they have been trained by an Alinsky method. The Left's goal is to have some trained socialist or liberal believers in every political office in every city, county, state, and national elected or appointed office.

For example, when I went on the school board, only two of the members had received the training to practice Alinsky's rule to isolate, freeze, and personalize the enemy. Someone or some conference had trained them in Alinsky's tactics early in their careers. The training had made them disciples, or "change agents." However, the other board members saw themselves as community leaders, having political ambitions or just wanting to help the community. They were liberal in their thinking, but not disciples. They yielded to the two leaders for fear of being attacked themselves and tried not to know too much. They were the lower-level foot soldiers, possessing little knowledge or power.

It's important to understand the levels of the socialist activists. I don't have a complete understanding of it, but just knowing there are levels of power and decision making will give you more power because you may be in a position that will require you to develop a strategy for each level. The highest rank is an elite group of highly educated and/or wealthy individuals who plan strategy. They coordinate plans of attack politically or in the press, although many campaigns against conservatives progress without much need for coordination. All those trained in Alinsky's rules have an innate ability to strike out without having to look for leadership. The tactics are second nature. The highest level keeps an eye on the continued progress of their control of the institutions with the most influence on the majority of Americans. They rule the high places of society.

The socialist elite are like generals in the army making goals and planning strategy, and they have ranks under them. The second level, the officers, has the job of accomplishing the elite's goals. The officers hold ranks similar to the army, from highest to lowest. The school board members who were trying to bring me down were lower-ranking officers. They had been trained to follow orders and rally others in local battles. The higher-level officers are those who have great hands-on power, such as those who used to work for the Clintons and now are advisers to Obama. They have as much power as those at the top and are elites as well, but they don't plan the highest level of strategy. I have been told they can be dangerous. One of my professors, a liberal researcher at the Hoover Institute, once cautioned me to be careful who I took on in the Culture War. He warned me, "There are evil people out there. You have to be careful." That was all he said, but it definitely struck me because he was a liberal and, although not a committed soldier, he knew the high-ranking officers.

The lowest-level soldiers are the rank and file. They are the foot soldiers in the unions, teachers in the classrooms, and your basic followers. Some of them are not aware of the depth of the war; they just want to get along, feel like good people, and feel important and useful. Those above them ramp them up at each election or when an effort is needed to keep someone out of office or remove someone from office. They can be the person who supports the efforts of the officers trying to get a Christian fired in the workplace. All they know is that there is an enemy and that they are the soldiers of righteousness. They are very motivated to keep Christians and conservatives out of institutions of power. I discovered this when one of my relatives was a leader in the teacher's union of the school district I served in. He was very zealous to keep me from winning and made many calls supporting the other candidates. He was disappointed when I won. Politics was thicker than relationship with that soldier.

In Alinsky's day, he mainly depended upon the Have-nots as his foot soldiers. However, today, we have more middle class than laboring class. In many areas of the country, the soldiers are middle class, but they have been convinced that conservatives have no compassion for the poorest. They have been manipulated to think that conservatives and Christians are hard-hearted.

Where you live in the country decides how many of the Left you will face. It also depends on the career God calls you to enter. If you live and work in the Bay Area, New York, or other Northeastern cities, you will feel very cautious about expressing your opinions on your job as well as publicly. Whatever strategy and tactics you use will depend upon where you live.

When Uncertain What to Say or Do— Pray, Pray, Pray

Remember, even if you don't have the experience, the Holy Spirit is creative and unpredictable. No one and no group can go outside of His experience. He has experienced every form of attack from the Enemy and has defeated him every time. The Holy Spirit is without an equal when it comes to accomplishing the will of the Father and Son while facing any obstacles. When I have been attacked throughout my life, meaning people have come against me or persecuted me for various reasons, I have always found that God never left me without a step-by-step strategy on how to overcome my opponents. It's astounding to me how many times the Lord has given specific directions on how to win a battle. He can confound any enemy. It's up to us to seek His guidance with faith and confidence until we receive an answer on how to proceed. God will not let His innocent servants be put to shame.

A Non-Alinsky Strategy

Alinsky is not the only one the Left looked to for strategies to secularize and socialize our culture. Other methods have been developed over the years when some new method was found to work. One that has worked and is difficult to disarm is the use of devious definitions. These definitions depend upon people making decisions based upon feelings instead of reason.

Recently Tammy Bruce, a conservative lesbian, practiced this method. She was talking on Fox about why homosexuals should be allowed to marry. She made a statement that used crafty language to confuse the public. She said that homosexuals were not redefining marriage; they were only adding others to the definition of marriage. In other words, if you said marriage is between a man and a woman or between a man and a man or between a woman and a woman, you were not redefining marriage, you were only broadening its scope. Now many Americans would have a sense that she was wrong, but without having any absolute truths with which to analyze it, they would find it difficult to resist. If they could not argue logically against the premise, then they would feel guilty to resist changing their minds.

How can we defuse this argument? First of all, we have to accept the premise that absolutes, or universal truths, exist. Then we have to accept the premise that the institution of marriage has a nature and that everything that exists has a nature. Dogs have dog characteristics or nature; pizza has pizza nature—consisting of various ingredients and a round shape; humans share human nature. Every created thing shares a nature with those of like kind.

From a Christian viewpoint, God created humans with human nature and their institutions evolve out of their nature. Marriage is an institution created by God to benefit His human creation. Marriage is based upon certain objective absolute standards that define it. These objective standards were established when God made Adam and Eve. Woman was made as man's helpmate and man was made with a need for a helpmate, just as humans were created with a need for God to complete them. He made them to complement— fit together—physically, emotionally, intellectually, and spiritually. They were designed to require either a human partner of the opposite sex or God himself to fulfill and complement them—fill in the empty places in their body, soul, and spirit. The marriage of a man and a woman is an intrinsic necessity built into their nature and into the nature of the marriage covenant. Scripture says it's even an example of the nature of Christ's relationship with His Church—the body of Christ—because it's our nature to need union with God. Humans cannot experience unity with any partner to the degree they achieve it with their husband or wife. Any other kind of union doesn't fit into the nature of marriage.

It's similar to the discussion earlier in the book about the intrinsic need of children for a father. Actually, we have to add the need for a mother to the intrinsic needs of children. Children are designed in such a way they cannot be whole without receiving the love from a father and a mother (or God as a substitute) to fill the places that are empty. It's the nature and design of children to require a father and mother's love to complete them. Two fathers or two mothers leaves out one person in each equation. Children will suffer feelings of incompleteness and anguish without both parents. It's the needs of their nature that require it. So, too, it's the needs of men and women based on their nature that leads them into making the covenant of marriage; any other covenant relationship that is called marriage is a violation of God's design.

If we remove God from the equations, we can argue from the nature of marriage. Again we fall back to all things have a nature. Everything that exists has a nature or characteristics that make it what it is. For example, butter has a butter nature. What is the nature of butter? It consists of cream and salt, whipped until it coagulates into butter. If saturated and nonsaturated fats were added to butter, it would no longer be butter. It would be more like margarine. Oils cannot be added to butter without an effect; they change its nature. So too, you cannot add other kinds of relationships to the marriage relationship and say you have not changed its nature. The nature of marriage is between a man and a woman. Any other kind of covenant relationship would have to be called something else—friendship, parents-children, lesbian, homosexual. Marriage cannot be broadened to include gays without changing its nature. You would no longer have marriage. If we change its nature, we must change its name. To call it "marriage" would be dishonest.

The constant pressure and undying effort used by radical homosexuals is one of Alinsky's strategies: "Maintain a constant pressure upon the opposition" and "If you push a negative hard and deep enough it will break through into its counterside. . ."[11]

The Left believes that if they refuse to surrender, they will achieve their goal. So far the strategy has worked. The only way to stop them is to show society the truth about their faulty reasoning. We have to appeal to the intellect of the people; we can no longer fight with emotion alone. Yes, our education system has removed absolutes, but we will have to restore them.

The only way to disarm deceptive arguments is to return to intellectual understanding of absolute truth. Jesus said He is the Way, the Truth and the Life, and He sent us the Spirit of Truth. The truth will set us free from the lies of our adversaries. What gays are now doing in their argument is no different than when the Left redefined the abortion issue. They told their opponents, the Christian Right, and the media that they could not be called "pro-abortion." They had to be called "pro-choice." Choice doesn't sound as bad as abortion, which has the connotation of murder. Christians were made to feel mean-spirited and angry if they continued to call pro-abortion advocates by their true names. Christians should have fought to keep the truth before the public and referred to themselves as anti-abortion (against murder) and their opposites as pro-abortion. Pro-life is also a valid term, but it should not exclude the anti-abortion label. Yes, we are for life, but we are also against murder.

In fact, science with its genetic discoveries and use of ultrasound has revealed the truth. Fetuses are babies and they are alive. The truth is gaining ground. The public is starting to respond to this truth by beginning to reject abortion. They know now that abortion is truly murder of a living being. Further connection should be made between the "right to choose" and the fact that the choice is not a choice; it's the act of taking the life of a baby, a living human being with a soul. In our attempt to restore absolute truth and absolute morality, we will have to define and apply the principles to every effort of the Left to justify their sins. We must return to standards, reason, and logic. We have to restore truth to our society. I don't have all the answers on how to accomplish this task, but this book is a beginning.

Guideline for Tactics and Strategy

One key guideline is to remain innocent. It was wrong for socialists to create a plan to deceive people through using the media, education, and other institution. Their goal is and was to confuse and deceive people, not inform and inspire them with the truth. Alinsky practiced and taught situational ethics. His thoughts on means and ends were as follows: *"To me ethics is doing what is best for the most."*[12] He went on to say that he would do whatever was necessary to win. These tactics are devilish and unworthy of any respect or admiration. We must never use these kinds of tactics. We must seek to spread God's truth through God's holy means. Our tactics will be positive efforts to bring truth and light.

On the job, we will have to live by high ethical standards. The truth and light have to do with our character. We need to be trustworthy and people of our word. We will have to be upright in what seems like a little thing, such as doing what we say or never taking something home from work. We should always go out of our way to help others and work well in a team setting. If someone has a personal problem, be ready to give advice or help. Give of your time and energy.

Besides being helpful and part of the group, also make an effort to do your very best. Be the one who has prepared or spent the extra time to be one of the best in the workplace, and then help others who want to improve as well. Never brag or think you are the best. Always remember that you can do nothing of any eternal value without Christ. Many times, Christians become proud of their goodness or abilities, but both are God-given. I try to remind myself when I start thinking I am somebody that I am actually nobody and should not expect any special treatment. I really am nobody without Christ. He has given me my talents and abilities and only through Him do they have any real value, eternally speaking, and do they function at their highest capacity. The Lord gives talents and fills them in with His Holy Spirit to make them excel. Ask God to make you the best that you can be on the job and in your character and give Him the glory when He answers your prayer.

The Culture Warriors of the past forty years created a plan that depended upon exposing the enemy, and that plan has had spotty success. Socialists have been able to turn the tables and judge some Christians and conservatives by their own rules. I believe formulating a new plan to reenter institutions and become influencers in those major institutions will enable us to restore our Judeo-Christian principles. When we effectively respond to socialist tactics and disarm them and don't sink to their level, it will confound our adversaries. Our strategy will remove the confusion most Americans live in.

Americans have been manipulated to allow socialists to determine their culture, but they don't agree in their hearts with the secular values that replaced the Judeo-Christian ones. They hate living in fear for the safety of their children. They hate the disorder of our society. They traded the physical safety of their children and the peace of their own consciences for the opportunity to have sexual freedom and determine their own values. Once they are presented with other choices, once the public realizes saying no to their flesh restores values that will guarantee a safer and more ordered and righteous society, they will welcome the restoration of Christian values to their culture.

How do I know that? I know people want the old values and standards because I see it every time I teach a class at the University of Phoenix. It's in the Central Valley of California, which is a more conservative area, but the students represent a cross-section of the majority of Americans. Many have fallen into going against their consciences as far as their sexual and drug activities and other self-gratifying behavior, but they are very unhappy with the consequences of their behavior in their personal lives and the culture. I teach history about the fifties, and students look longingly back to that period because of its safety and greater innocence. In their essays, they express their fear for the safety of their children, especially having to do with sexual predators, and in the problems they will face when their children become teenagers.

Once Christians understand moral absolutes and objective truth, they can and will convey these principles to society. Communicating these truths and values will provide the missing knowledge that leaves my students and other Americans feeling powerless and dissatisfied. Most Americans are ready to gravitate back to those values; they just need help. Once they understand that restoring Judeo-Christian principles will restore a protective environment for them and their children, I believe they will be ready to give up their lawless practices.

Before Christians can transfer knowledge about moral absolutes and objective truth, they will have to be educated in those principles first. Of course this information is not taught in public schools and even many Christian schools don't have courses teaching these principles. Moral absolutes and objective truth are the Judeo-Christian principles missing from our culture. They are God's mind and morals revealed to mankind. Christians will need to understand them before they can restore them to the culture. The next chapter will pass on this missing knowledge to the generations who have missed it and to the next generation.

CHAPTER NINE

Restoring Moral Absolutes and Reasoning

Scene: a University classroom. The debate for the night was the pros and cons of gay "marriage." The emotional debate rose and fell as personal feelings became more passionate. John was the thinker in the class and had been raised with traditional and Christian values. Restrained but determined, John stepped into the debate:

He quietly but firmly explained, "The moral state of our society is deteriorating and gay marriage would throw the society into greater moral chaos, and religion would become obsolete."

Mercedes responded excitedly, "Religion has nothing to do with the issue of gay marriage. The First Amendment says religion cannot enter into social and political decisions. Religion can't be used as an argument."

John cautiously continued to press his point, not wanting to offend Mercedes, "Gays can still have relationships; they just shouldn't marry. Christianity and Christian traditions have defined marriage for centuries. How can you throw out these moral ideas without considering the consequences to society?"

Mercedes paused and wrestled in her mind. Stumped but undaunted she shifted into an intimate moment with the class: "I have a wife," she declared. "I am married to a woman, and I married for love, not for money or anything else, just love. I want to live with this person for the rest of my life and help raise her son. Why shouldn't I be able to marry the person I love just as a heterosexual can?"

At that point the debate ended. She had not won, but no one could say anything else against gay marriage without rebuffing and denying her feelings. Her feelings determined her morality, and no one could tell her she was wrong. Once her feelings were expressed, reasoning became a weapon, not a tool. Reason no longer mattered. It was now personal.

After the debate, I carefully discussed principles and concepts that thinkers use to make moral decisions. I could not bring in the principles of natural and unnatural or our founders' distinction between religion and a state church (denomination). In order to avoid conflicts and false accusations of prejudice, I had to avoid some very important moral principles and intellectual tools.

Our society has come to the point in which most of my students, who I believe are a cross-section of a majority of Americans in the twenty- to forty-year-old range, have no understanding of moral absolutes or how to reason. They discuss and make important life decisions based upon feelings. They shift from one side of an argument to the other without realizing they are being illogical. The suffering of most Americans is very great; they are troubled in their hearts and minds and don't have any idea how to release themselves from bondage. Which brings us to the question: Who or what in our nation is most responsible for allowing its people to be brainwashed and enticed into such an immoral and irrational state?

In the process of my writing this book, God has clarified for me the major cause for that revolution. It has been the failure of churches to pass on America's Judeo-Christian intellectual and moral traditions. They didn't defend and retain those principles adequately against secular radicals. Since our ancestors introduced Protestant values and standards, it's the Protestant churches more than any other who have failed our nation and our national calling. As mentioned in chapter six, most Protestants either joined the secularists with intellectual dishonesty or turned to emotion and experience rather than reason. The latter acted weakly and withdrew from society into Christian isolation. Both failed to be good stewards.

As a result of losing our moral traditions, our society and people are broken. Many people come to the Lord in a broken state, having been brutally damaged by the sins of their parents or by their own sinful acts. Since they have not been raised with knowledge of right and wrong, they have suffered appalling psychological and emotional damage. They live enslaved to the consequences of sins. Pastors spend most of their time and most of the church ministries aimed at healing and rebuilding broken lives. The Christian army is crippled and pastors become burnt out trying to make them into effective soldiers in God's kingdom.

The reason for the burnout is that many pastors emphasize the healing and transformation of the heart and emotions to the neglect of the mind. Healing of the heart is just one side of the coin that makes a healthy, balanced, and knowledgeable Christian. Believers' ability to use their intellect and reason in order to know and defend their faith makes them spiritually stronger and more stable. Even having a close relationship with the Lord requires intellectual understanding of biblical concepts and doctrines. Paul's letter to the Romans includes deep spiritual insights, which require study and teaching for understanding.

One way to overcome the breakdown in American society is to reintroduce Christians (yes, Christians first) to their intellectual and moral heritage. The conscience cannot be touched without understanding. The mind is involved in the process of a conviction and repentance. If the mind is sloppy because it's taught more about moral relativism than moral absolutes, then the conscience cannot receive conviction for sin. Moral relativism leads to vacant minds and uninformed consciences. The mind has to be sharpened and trained in order to bring people back to moral truths.

The book *Love Your God with All of Your Mind* by J.P. Moreland has some solid recommendations to restore reasoning and logic to church teachings. He defines faith as "a power or skill to act in accordance with the nature of the kingdom of God, a trust in what we have reason to believe is true."[1] He continues, "If this is correct, then sermons should target people's thinking as much as their wills and feelings."[2] He believes that "faith is built on reason." I recommend that many of his suggestions be applied and followed in churches. In addition, we have to remember that the Nicene Creed mentions there is one "catholic" church, which means there is one universal church (body of Christ) with universal doctrines all Christians should know.

These doctrines were developed before the "catholic" church became the Roman Catholic Church. Christians should be familiar with the teachings of the early fathers and with later reformers in the Roman Catholic Church who have illuminating, scholarly teachings and devotionals, such as St. Francis of Assisi, Teresa of Ávila, John of the Cross, and Thomas à Kempis. Then we have Protestant thinkers like Andrew Murray, Watchman Nee, C. S. Lewis, and John Donne. In addition, classical literature has wonderful examples of moral choices and consequences and most of them are Christian except those of the early Greeks and Romans. These are only a few writers Christians could read to sharpen their spirits and minds. There are a large number of sources to provide for intellectual and spiritual growth.

This chapter will provide a means to renew the mind—it will introduce the reader to ways to think rationally. Its purpose is to demonstrate logical and rational thinking. I am not presenting classical reasoning in its higher form. This is just an introduction to reasoning on a fundamental level since most Christians have not had much exposure to critical or logical thinking. Churches or Christian colleges can use this book to initiate learning through workshops and internships, and I encourage any church that uses this book as the curriculum for a training program to go beyond it and add some of your own favorite authors. In addition, the reader can draw from it personally for your own edification. The next section will explain and demonstrate in layman's terms how to develop reasoning skills.

Examples of Reasoning

Reasoning is a faculty of the mind and is necessary for spiritual growth. Since God is all-knowing, we, too, have the capacity to gain knowledge and use our intellects. Man is an intellectual being made in God's image and likeness. We all have the faculty of reasoning because we have a mind. In order to use the faculty, with God's guidance of course, we need to think using universal principles. We need to rediscover ideas like nature, substance, essence, and standards. In reading philosophy and theology, we would need to know these principles in a highly intellectual form, but for this book, we are going to try to keep it intellectual but simple. I am not a theologian or a philosopher, but I have found we can follow logical reasoning to important godly conclusions. When we seek understanding, God can open our minds to understand the source of truth. The following information will lay a foundation for learning how to reason.

There are two kinds of classical approaches to logical reasoning: deductive and inductive reasoning.

Deductive Reasoning

In deductive reasoning, a person reasons or thinks through an intellectual argument from a known truth. For example, the majority of people would agree through experience that human nature is not good. It's some mixture of good and evil. In other words, most people believe that children are born with tendencies to do some wrong things if not prevented from doing so by their parents and later by society's laws. Christians refer to this state of human nature, being identified after Adam and Eve sinned, as "sin nature." The Catholic Church calls it the "state of original sin." Some modern thinkers believe that human nature is basically good, and society corrupts it. Whichever idea dominates people's thinking will determine how they raise their children, handle their relationships, and choose their preferred kind of government.

Now we will go through the reasoning process to apply the interpretation of human nature to the resulting kinds of government. If human nature is perceived as good, then the government proceeding from that belief will be much different from a government formulated on the belief that human nature has a tendency to sin.

Some thinkers throughout the ages have believed that human nature is basically good and society and the environment corrupt it and cause people to act uncivilized. The way to create a peaceful society is to have government provide for the needs of the people, removing poverty. In this way of thinking, justice means that everyone is guaranteed a comfortable life whether they work for it or not. In this kind of society, in which no one has unfulfilled material needs, people will behave unselfishly. There would be no envy and without envy there would be no reason to steal from or murder someone for having something you don't have.

If you take it another step and decide the government is the tool to provide for everyone's needs, then it will establish institutions to provide the basic needs and care for every child. For example, the state will justify removing children from their homes and from their parents to provide what the state deems the correct environment. Parental rights will be undermined. State-run schools will contradict parental values, such as parents no longer having the right to know if their daughter has an abortion. They will concentrate on emotional and physical needs rather than educate their students' minds, which happened in the United States from the 1960s to the 1990s with the emphasis on self-esteem to the neglect of learning. All the above is an example of the state molding society to fit its view of human nature.

As mentioned in chapter one, socialists deduced this conclusion based upon socialists' view that human nature is good. The final goal of socialism is communism, which would create a society in which there would be no need for government because the state had provided for everyone according to need. In this scenario, the expectation is that since people are basically good, they will now do the right thing and help each other without interference or punishment from the state.

This theory was tested by a professor in a classroom experiment. He wanted to see if all the smarter students would continue to work hard to provide good grades for everyone else. He was testing the goodness of human nature.

Experiment with Socialism, Socialism gets an F

An economics professor at Texas Tech said he had never failed a single student, but had once failed an entire class.

The class (students) insisted that socialism worked since no one would be poor and no one would be rich, a great equalizer. The professor then said, "OK, we will have an experiment in this class on socialism."

"All grades will be averaged and everyone will receive the same grade so no one will fail and no one will receive an A."

After the first test the grades were averaged and everyone got a B. The students who had studied hard were upset while the students who had studied very little were happy.

But, as the second test rolled around, the students who had studied little studied even less and the ones who had studied hard decided that since they couldn't make an A, they also studied less. The second test average was a D.

No one was happy. When the third test rolled around the average grade was an F.

The scores never increased as bickering, blame, name-calling all resulted in hard feelings and no one would study for anyone else.

To their great surprise all failed. The professor told them that socialism would ultimately fail because the harder people try to succeed the greater their reward (capitalism) but when a government takes all the reward away (socialism) no one will try or succeed.[3]

Now according to socialist thinking, since human nature is good, the students earning As and Bs should have happily agreed to give their points to the other students without resentment (this can be applied economically). Of course, the flaw in socialist thinking is obvious. Since those getting higher grades would be denied their just reward, they would stop trying to get good grades. It reveals a flaw and naïveté in socialist thinking about human nature.

Now let us look at the kind of government that is deduced from the belief that human nature is burdened with original sin. The basic understanding is that even if society were perfect in every way and there were no injustices and no poverty (an impossible scenario), people, because of sin nature, would still have envy, anger, hatred, and jealousy. They would still steal, murder, and commit other sins and other crimes. Therefore, the goal of those who create a government founded upon this understanding of human nature would mainly be to keep order and provide the rule of law. The goal of government would not be first and foremost to provide everything people needed, but to provide a society in which everyone has equal opportunity to meet their needs. However, it doesn't mean the state would turn a blind eye to poverty and disadvantage; it just means it would provide the means for improvement, not become the caretaker.

When a government is created with sin nature in focus, the founders of that government are aware that too much power given to one person or any group of people would lead to tyranny and the loss of the rule of law. Here is the thinking: The problem is that you cannot trust one person with absolute power, a few people with absolute power, the majority with absolute power, or any branch of government with absolute power. In order to preserve human rights and justice, you would have to create a government in which the people have a great deal of power, but the government would have control of the people if they became lawless. However, you also would have to find a way to keep government from wielding so much power that it would become dictatorial.

Different nations have developed different balances of power to try to solve this problem. America was the first to truly tackle the problem in an ingenious way and that is why it became the model—a City on a Hill. To keep it short, since our goal is to understand deductive reasoning, not provide a civics lesson, we will look at a shortened version of our constitutional setup. Our Founding Fathers' solution was to check, or keep under control, everyone's sin nature. For example, we have a democracy, but the people vote for representatives; they don't vote directly for every law. It's a republican, democratic system, not a direct democracy. In other words, the people don't have absolute control of political decisions because the representatives can vote according to their own preferences. Of course, the people can vote them out of office in the next election, but in the meantime, the will of the majority is postponed.

Besides the sin nature of the people being controlled in our system, the sin nature of the representatives is also controlled by the checks and balances and separation of powers of the three branches of government. No one branch has total power; their powers overlap. The states also have certain guaranteed rights that keep the federal government from becoming all controlling. In our system of government, the problem of sinful human nature is solved without needing one ruler or a few rulers controlling every element of society as long as the setup created by the Constitution is not ignored or misinterpreted.

What we have done in this exercise is use deductive reasoning, starting with the premise of how one views human nature. Each viewpoint leads to certain unavoidable conclusions if you follow logic and reason. Of course, this has been somewhat simplistic but hopefully an effective example. As a reader, you might want to practice some other deductive reasoning. Here are a few other exercises to tackle:

- How does free will answer the question of evil in this world? Here are some guidelines for your reasoning process: You would describe free will, the problems arising from it, God's relationship to it, and how free will is related to evil.
- Another exercise in deductive reasoning is: Since God created moral laws, what are the consequences when people disobey them? It's helpful to relate moral laws to physical laws, such as the law of gravity.

Inductive Reasoning

Inductive reasoning starts with observation of many facts or mini-truths that result in ascertaining a universal truth. For example, the observation of the universe and the laws that rule the universe is a good place to start. Science reveals there are certain physical laws that keep the universe in order. "The theory of intelligent design holds that certain features of the universe and of living things are best explained by an intelligent cause, not an undirected process such as natural selection."[4] The life-sustaining physical architecture of the universe alone, without even considering biological or geological information, reveals a designer. Even further, humans are able to harness these laws to provide light for our homes, signals for our cell phones, and principles for multiple kinds of modern transportation. The stream of physical laws is endless.

Anyone with an open, unprejudiced mind has to ask the question whether it's possible for this ordered universe to be the result of disorder. Can it be possible that these physical laws are not really laws but an evolutionary accident? Most people have enough common sense to know there must be an intelligent designer behind the creation of such a planned, universal set of laws. There has to be a designer who can think, plan, and create. If there is such a designer, what else can you call Him except God, the Creator of all things?

Aristotle was considered the first philosopher/physicist to describe and practice inductive reasoning. He studied organisms, humans, and human societies to formulate final causes. The reader can follow the same path, choosing certain fields to study and from which to draw conclusions. For example, you could write down observations about a friend's or family's behavior for a week and draw conclusions from the observations. Or study the science of DNA and draw some universal conclusions. Besides deductive and inductive reasoning, moral absolutes are a part of moral reasoning.

Moral Absolutes

Why is knowledge of moral absolutes important? It's important because moral laws exist. And yes, we experience the painful consequences of violating them whether we know them or not. Thankfully, God in His mercy has provided forgiveness, but we carry the memory of our sins, and we will have to battle the condemnation from demons or our own regrets many times throughout our lives. In addition, we could suffer ongoing negative results from our sins, such as physical or emotional damage. For example, sexual sins could lead to out-of-wedlock pregnancy or a sexual disease.

So far in this chapter we have practiced deductive and inductive reasoning. Now we will apply the two techniques to discovering universal ethical principles that guide behavior.

We will begin the search for moral absolutes based upon nature—God's nature and man's nature. When we study God's character, or nature, we discover the Judeo-Christian ethical system.

His ethical system is an extension of His nature. Our moral excellence is dependent upon knowing God's moral excellence. First, God's nature is moral and holy. He is pure and free from all sin. God's moral qualities are the ones that give us moral guidance for our lives. He is our example and Jesus is the manifestation of that example. The Bible says God's nature is love, and that is the highest principle of morality. Love embraces all moral principles. When Christians have unconditional love, they will manifest God's moral qualities of honesty, obedience, kindness, reliability, trustworthiness, thoughtfulness, discretion, justice, graciousness, etc. That is why Jesus said that the two main Commandments are to love God and one's neighbor. When we love God and our neighbor, we will be moral because our nature has been conformed to His.

As mentioned above, when Adam and Eve sinned, they introduced sin into our nature, causing sin nature. Adam and Eve still reflected God's image by having a desire to be good and retaining other godly qualities, but they could no longer succeed in being perfectly good. God then began a journey, using people and events in history to prepare the way for restoration. The Father's goal was to provide a means of forgiveness for sin in order to prevent justice from requiring all people be separated from Him forever. Of course, He sent His Son to pay the price for our sins.

The Ten Commandments revealed the sin nature and sins which the Son died to wash away. God introduced the Ten Commandments to reveal the moral laws that ruled God's moral system of justice. These laws revealed man's sin nature because people, having sin nature, could not obey all of them and suffered painful consequences for their disobedience. It was His way of preparing for the more perfect law of love found in the New Testament. He used the Ten Commandments to reveal the moral absolutes He required all His children to obey. These moral laws were and continue to be the laws that govern moral behavior, just as physical laws govern the physical behavior of planets, stars, and galaxies. When these moral laws are broken there are automatic consequences. God doesn't suddenly intervene and punish someone; instead, one's actions trigger a consequence only God's mercy can prevent.

We will review the Ten Commandments to understand God's expectations from His children and His moral laws. The Ten Commandments help define the moral laws that have been written on the hearts of believers and that are summed up in what James called the "royal law," mentioned above. The Ten Commandments reveal many more moral teachings and requirements than we identify on first reading. You have to reflect on each Commandment to realize the ramification for moral teachings and ethical behavior. They are an expression of God's nature and help define His moral laws.

Let us delve into the Commandments to find their broader meaning. The first and second Commandments speak to you about putting God first, having no other gods before Him and not making any gods. At first, you may only see that God doesn't want you to put your possessions, another person, or anything else created before your worship of Him. Things and people easily become idols. However, if you analyze those two Commandments, you will find other moral qualities God is asking us to acquire. In fact, you cannot obey those Commandments without developing other moral qualities. For example, you cannot obey them without becoming faithful, trustworthy, dependable, loyal, and reliable.

When you are told to have no other gods, God is asking you to be faithful. God is faithful and He never breaks His promises. So, too, God wants you to acquire the quality of faithfulness so you can serve Him all your life and not break your promises. However, faithfulness to God is only the beginning. You are also called to be a faithful husband, wife, parent, child, friend, and employee to whomever you have made a commitment to. The moral quality of faithfulness stands above many others.

One example of faithfulness relates to the seventh Commandment, "You shall not commit adultery." God expects you to be faithful to the promise you made when you married your spouse. Jesus even expanded the requirement to avoid adultery when, in the Sermon on the Mount, He said that even looking at someone and lusting after that person is committing adultery in your heart.

All of us have to stay faithful when we are attracted to people to whom we are not married. There could be someone in the workplace or in a school situation. We see them every day and find it hard to remain faithful, or we have to be careful not even to flirt with that person much less have sex. Yes, we might have flirted one time because it was an unexpected reaction on our part. But after that one time, it should not happen again. It takes great determination and commitment to the Lord and to our spouses to avoid sin. The people we are attracted to will not become gods if we have faithfulness lodged in our heart and mind through reading the Word and prayer. God will honor our faithfulness to Him by giving us the power to be faithful to others.

Another quality that relates to faithfulness is trustworthiness. God trusts us to worship only Him. He expects us to play by the rules and keep our promises. When we promise Him or another person we will do something, we must do what we say in order to keep our promise. We should not make promises lightly. Often we want to please people, and we will agree to do something to which we should not have committed. We should stop ourselves and think before we make a promise. If we cannot fulfill a promise, we should not make it. It's a very common practice for people to say they will do something and have no intention to do it. I can usually tell the people who make promises without their hearts being in it. I just don't depend on them, and sadly, I am almost always right about them. When people put their trust in us, we must not fail them. We don't want them to have misplaced their trust.

Of course we can see that once we commit to obeying the first two Commandments, we cannot obey them without acquiring many other excellent moral qualities such as those mentioned above. It's the same for the other Commandments.

The third Commandment tells us not to take God's name in vain. What does that mean? How is that a moral issue? At the time the Commandments were given, God's name was used to guarantee an oath or promise. If someone used His name and broke his promise, it was a sign of disrespect of God. His name would be used in vain, and it exposed a lack of respect, esteem, and reverence toward God. The opposite of taking His name in vain is to reverence and honor Him. Those are the moral qualities that arise out of the third Commandment. We reverence God because His attributes are so far beyond anything we can achieve. His activities and morality are superior in every way to our own.

When we have respect, reverence, and honor for God and all authority, we are acting according to the moral law. If we consider these moral qualities further, we can see they also lead to gratitude, which is one of the most important moral qualities. Gratefulness is a natural response to God's goodness. We cannot honor His goodness and mercy without feeling grateful. When we're grateful, we don't blame God for struggles and suffering; we learn to trust Him and thank Him for everything. Without thankfulness we cannot grow spiritually. We will disconnect from God and fall into sin or become self-righteous and legalistic.

Gratitude is a moral quality because it's the other side of humility. People cannot feel appreciation toward someone who has helped them if they are proud. Pride would say the other person or God didn't do enough. In today's culture, most people feel very special. Many think their lives and happiness are more important than pleasing God or serving others. Therefore, pride and self-pity keep them from appreciating acts of kindness and blessings from God and others. Pride, lack of gratitude, and self-pity cause many deaths in gang-infested communities and increase acts of suicide and enslavement to addictions.

The fourth Commandment says, "Observe the Sabbath day, to keep it holy." Remembering the Sabbath is also a moral law. The original celebration of the Sabbath reminded Israel of all God had done for them and His requirement they worship only Him. The New Testament broadened the idea of the fourth Commandment to mean we should always rest in Him for everything and every accomplishment (see Gal. 2:20). We don't do things for God; God accomplishes His purposes through us. We pray and supplicate with thanksgiving, waiting upon Him for the answer. Resting in the Lord is an act of faith and trust. The Israelites were criticized for having evil hearts of unbelief. In other words, faith is a virtue and lack of faith is a sin.

Once we have faith in God to fulfill His plan, we need humility to let Him guide us. He will reveal every step to take and reassure us when we're tempted to take action on our own. If we take action outside of God's timing and will, we will become prideful. God may still bless the work, but, in time, our pride will push us to step outside of God's will to do our own projects. Those projects will become tiring and lead to exhaustion. Our own physical and emotional limitations will finally end our pride and bring us back to humility. That's an example of the consequences of violating God's moral law about the Sabbath.

> For if Joshua had given them rest, then He would not afterward have spoken of another day. There remains therefore a rest for the people of God. For he who has entered His rest has himself also ceased from his works as God *did* from His. Let us therefore be diligent to enter that rest, lest anyone fall according to the same example of disobedience. For the word of God *is* living and powerful, and sharper than any two-edged sword, piercing even to the division of soul and spirit, and of joints and marrow, and is a discerner of the thoughts and intents of

the heart. And there is no creature hidden from His sight, but all things *are* naked and open to the eyes of Him to whom we *must give* account. (Heb. 4:8–13)

The fifth Commandment says, "Honor your father and your mother." Of course many moral principles can be derived from this Commandment. The greatest act of honor to authority is obedience. Even Jesus learned obedience through the things He suffered. Even He had to be obedient to His Heavenly Father and to His earthly father and mother. Of course, if your parents or spouse asked you to sin or reject God, then you cannot be obedient. However, such a situation doesn't occur very often. Therefore, obedience is one of the most important moral laws.

God rejected Saul as king because he didn't obey Him. Samuel told him obedience was more important than sacrifice. We can find that in our lives as well. Sometimes we can deceive ourselves by doing good works when God is asking us to do something else. We can avoid God's request by doing some service for the church, or work for an individual. Often God will ask us to spend more time with our family or with Him. It's most important to be obedient in order to please Him.

As we have seen, multiple moral and ethical principles can be expanded from the Ten Commandments. The reader can deduce the rest from the remaining five Commandments. The greatest commandment is the one Jesus declared to the question, 'Teacher, which is the greatest commandment in the Law?' Jesus replied: "'Love the Lord your God with all your heart and with all your soul and with all your mind.' This is the first and greatest commandment. And the second is like it: "Love you neighbor as yourself." All the Law and the Prophets hang on these two commandments.'" (Matt. 22:36–40 NIV). What Jesus was saying was that from these two commandments we can deduce all others. They contain the Ten Commandments and even more of His moral laws. It's only a matter of using the Word to explore all the qualities of God's nature and how His teachings define the moral laws that rule our behavior toward each other and toward God. These moral laws are absolute; they're not relative.

In addition to loving God with our hearts, Jesus expressed the importance of loving God with our minds. It reveals the importance of our minds. In order to expand our knowledge of how the mind works, we will practice another exercise for the mind. We will apply godly principles to different moral dilemmas we all face in our lives.

Application of Moral Principles

First, let us look at the spiritual and rational reasons behind God's clear instructions in the Bible that a man and woman should not have sex before marriage.

Sadly, fornication is extremely common in many churches. The world causes people to feel they are being abnormal if they remain virgins until marriage. Therefore, because of the secular influence, many Christians have taken this sin very lightly. Paul instructs we are temples of the Holy Spirit and that when we unite with another person, we become one flesh with him or her. By becoming one flesh with someone outside of marriage, we have brought disorder into our lives. We have changed God's order for relationships and commitments and profaned what is sacred.

> Flee sexual immorality. Every sin that a man does is outside the body, but he who commits sexual immorality sins against his own body. Or do you not know that your body is the temple of the Holy Spirit *who is* in you, whom you have from God, and you are not your own? For you were bought at a price; therefore glorify God in your body and in your spirit, which are God's. (1 Cor. 6:18–20)

Remember, all of God's creation has a certain order, whether physical, moral, spiritual, or biological. When one violates this order, pain is the consequence. In the moral order, the pain can be emotional, of the heart, and physical. When people practice sex outside of marriage, if they have a sensitive conscience, they suffer feelings of guilt and shame. If the relationship doesn't end in marriage, the time of healing and recuperation is much longer than with a relationship in which sex was not part of the relationship. Both usually feel used, frustrated, condemned, a failure, and unsettled. It takes time to restore health and normal self-esteem. Some people may feel it had no effect, but it's impossible, except for sociopaths, to have no wounding of the heart, mind, and emotions.

Marriage was created by God for many reasons. First, He revealed in Ephesians 5 that marriage is a covenant action that symbolizes His relationship with His church, His bride. "For we are members of His body, of His flesh and of His bones. *'For this reason a man shall leave his father and mother and be joined to his wife, and the two shall become one flesh.'* This is a great mystery, but I speak concerning Christ and the church" (Eph. 5:30–32)

Marriage has a very sacred connotation and holds a high responsibility to reflect His relationship to His bride. Sex is an expression of that union. When a man and woman make a marriage covenant, they have become one—spirit, soul, and body have intermingled in unity. The marriage covenant binds the man and woman in all aspects of their being; one aspect, such as the body, or sex, cannot be disconnected from the others and united with someone before marriage without dishonoring God's perfect plan.

As we can see, sex outside of marriage dishonors God's plan and intentions. It pulls the body from its proper place in relation to its own soul and spirit as well as with the spiritual meaning of marriage and twists it to fit the dominance of the flesh. It dishonors God's design for sexuality and profanes the purpose of sex. In the process, a Christian not only commits the sin of fornication but also sins by failing to be trustworthy, reliable, dependable, faithful, loyal, and obedient to God.

The sin of adultery involves sexual sin, but with adultery, the sin is not just a violation of a person's covenant with God, it's also a violation of the covenant a person has made with his or her spouse. It has greater ramifications and brings greater disorder in God's design. If there are children, it causes dysfunction in the whole family. The adulterer can try to prevent his or her spouse and the family from suffering the pain and consequence of his or her sin, but there will usually be some sinful reaction to an ungodly action.

Another common sin is lying. This sin has been diminished and devalued by today's culture. People lie with a wink and a smirk, making it appear harmless and acceptable. Someone who is a liar won't get into heaven. Why is it wrong? The Holy Spirit is the Spirit of Truth. Truth is an important aspect of God's character. Truth, the Word, and Light are all names used to identify God. We are dependent upon God being truthful to be able to depend upon His promises. Since we are made in His image and likeness and saved by His blood, we are obligated to live in the Light. We cannot live the darkness of deception and lies.

Satan uses lies to deceive us and entice us to sin. He knows that by using deception he can cause confusion and disorder. He and his demons form plans against us, trying to cause us to sin and then trick us into lying about what we have done, adding sin upon sin. The more we lie the more we harden our hearts against God. Then our consciences cannot be touched by God, and we become numb to guilt and shame. Satan's tactics keep us from salvation, or if we are saved, take us away from God.

In order to grow close to God, we have to be honest and truthful. We have to be like him and keep our word. If we commit to something or make a promise, it's required of us to fulfill our word. If we are not trustworthy, we cannot represent God's character to others. We are dependent upon God being true to His word for our salvation. He keeps His promises because He is Truth; He never lies. If He lied, we could not trust Him to do what He says He will do. Then our lives would be in chaos and complete disorder.

As you can see from the analysis above, using revelation and reason, we can apply God's moral principles to our lives. We can see why He commands us to duplicate His moral character by obeying His moral laws. Only when we are being obedient can we live in peace and unity with Him, others, and ourselves.

Jesus honored the Law and when we follow the spirit of the Law, we are pleasing God. Our age needs to know the deeper meaning of the Law as it reveals God's excellent character and His will for our lives. It will inform our consciences to keep us from taking sin lightly.

Do not think that I came to destroy the Law or the Prophets. I did not come to destroy but to fulfill. For assuredly, I say to you, till heaven and earth pass away, one jot or one tittle will by no means pass from the law till all is fulfilled. Whoever therefore breaks one of the least of these commandments, and teaches men so, shall be called least in the kingdom of heaven; but whoever does and teaches *them*, he shall be called great in the kingdom of heaven. For I say to you, that unless your righteousness exceeds *the righteousness* of the scribes and Pharisees, you will by no means enter the kingdom of heaven. (Matt. 5:17–20)

Personal Example

In the 1950s, the majority of people accepted Christian moral standards without question. They believed they needed a moral standard and that the Judeo-Christian standard was the best one. It didn't mean that everyone obeyed those standards. People violated the standards often, but the fact that there was an agreed-upon morality held back some of the dishonesty and crime that would have increased without it.

For example, while in high school, we all accepted moral teachings about sex before marriage. Many of the boys were wired to try, but most of the girls said no. The feeling of guilt and shame and what people would say kept many students from having sex. It may not have been from spiritual motives, but it worked to keep some young people from suffering major negative consequences as many youth experience today. There were not as many illegitimate children, sexual diseases, single mothers, and poor families.

Of course, some of my friends did have sex and suffered from feeling guilty. However, if they had known the Lord, they could have moved beyond that guilt to forgiveness and cleansing. Instead, many of them hardened their hearts because they identified with the feminists in the sixties, denying guilt and shame in order to have sexual freedom. Seeking power and self-gratification, they removed the Judeo-Christian moral constraints about sex.

Dennis Prager, a journalist and thinker who practices Judaism, has a series of articles that encapsulates Judeo-Christian values in relation to the secular view of the twentieth and twenty-first centuries. When you go to his Web site, click on the year 2005. He has a number of articles on the subject on his website: http://townhall.com/columnists/. Here is an excerpt from "The case for Judeo-Christian values: Part II":

> For those who subscribe to Judeo-Christian values, right and wrong, good and evil, are derived from God, not from reason alone, nor from the human heart, the state or through majority rule.
>
> Though most college-educated Westerners never hear the case for the need for God-based morality because of the secular outlook that pervades modern education and the media, the case is both clear and compelling: If there is no transcendent source of morality (morality is the word I use for the standard of good and evil), "good" and "evil" are subjective opinions, not objective realities.
>
> In other words, if there is no God who says, "Do not murder" ("Do not kill" is a mistranslation of the Hebrew which, like English, has two words for homicide), murder is not wrong. Many people may think it is wrong, but that is their opinion, not objective moral fact. There are no moral "facts" if there is no God; there are only moral opinions.[5]

Another example of how our society has lost "God-based morality" is the state laws that allow minor children to obtain abortions without parental consent. It involves the universal principles of parental rights, yet the majority is being manipulated to think that parental rights are a matter of opinion rather than a guaranteed right. It's part of the socialist attack on the institution of the family because control of families means control of the nation. When the state overrides the rights of parents, they raise the children. Then the state controls the children's beliefs, thoughts, and ethics. It has complete control of the people because, as the children mature, it will have complete control of its citizens' minds.

The Supreme Court has recently fallen into confusion about parental rights. Since the Constitution doesn't mention them, the court has lost sight of the classic philosophical as well as scriptural roots of the importance of the family. Parental rights were not introduced into the Constitution because the Founding Fathers considered them a given. Families existed before societies; in fact families were the first social unit. Societies consist of a combination of all families. Without families we have no people and therefore no citizens, society, or government. Parental rights are imbedded in universal traditions and practices that establish the rights of the family over the rights of the state. For example, the state recognizes this position by the law that doesn't allow the state to enter a family's home without a court order from a judge. Their rights are protected from the state.

Because the family is the source of the state's existence, family rights are primary and the government's laws are secondary. The families, or the people, choose to relinquish certain rights to the state; the state cannot arbitrarily increase its reach without the people's agreement. The state depends upon the family for the scope of its power; it cannot breach the primary power of the family (the citizens) without good reason and legal justification. According to our Declaration of Independence, all rights come from God, not the government. God gives inalienable rights to people, not the state. What God has given cannot indiscriminately be taken away by the state. Why? Because the state was created to protect the peoples' rights, not promote its own power.

Fit parents have the right and responsibility to make life-or-death and life-changing choices for their minor children. Children don't have the capacity to make adult decisions until they are adults. Parents by blood or adoption have the responsibility to guide and protect their children, even from the state when necessary. The state cannot violate the rights of parents to protect their children from physical and emotional harm. They, not the state, bear that responsibility first unless they are proved unfit parents.

Recently, the public has been manipulated to believe that parental rights need to be breached to protect minor children from their abusive parents. The propositions put on the ballot to reverse the laws against parental rights failed twice in California. The public could not even understand that the initiatives have a built-in protection for children. The socialist ideas have penetrated people's understanding about rights and freedom. When more people lose control of their children to the state, they may wake up. Any parent knows that the state must not have the right to make decisions for them with such issues as abortion. Since children are not mature enough to do the right thing, they must turn to their parents. The state needs to promote and encourage children to turn to their parents for help. But instead, the state is working to undermine parental authority. And children will always seek the authority that will feed their independence and self-gratification. It's one more battle Culture Warriors need to win by bringing back the principles that will remove the blinders from our citizens' minds.

The loss of Judeo-Christian principles has resulted in what the British thinker G. K. Chesterton stated at the turn of the twentieth century: "When a Man stops believing in God he doesn't then believe in nothing, he believes in anything."[6] Culture Warriors need to know how to reason and use their intellect, and then they will be able to present moral absolutes in such a way as to make them the source of enlightenment to their secular fellow employees and friends. Christian believers should be able to reason from nature and moral laws without necessarily introducing God into the equation. Common sense, reason, and human experience can verify moral principles. For example, Christians know God's scriptural rebuke of fornication, but it can be related in a form of cautioning to a secular friend.

A warrior can bring up how once a couple has sex, the relationship moves into a different stage. Everyone pursuing a more permanent relationship understands how sex causes new dimensions in a relationship. Confusion and fear can follow the act—fear of betrayal and abandonment—and expectations for a deeper commitment rise up. One or both feel a tugging on their hearts to give and expect more. That is why some people nowadays try to avoid sex until they know the other has the potential to become a spouse. The feeling of a need for a deeper commitment after sex reveals how God's moral laws are still in charge of people's actions, even if they don't follow God's order.

A Culture Warrior can use these kinds of insights to return God's principles to the culture. We can see that many people's consciences are still informed by Judeo-Christian principles. Most people cannot avoid feeling and responding to God's moral laws. When someone points out the reason for those feelings, that there are principles of right and wrong that cannot be ignored, it can make sense to them. Remember, they have been manipulated by the Left to ignore their consciences, but it's not really possible. People feel guilty and need a way out of their guilt and truly want out of their continuous suffering for violating God's moral laws. Many are dissatisfied with self-gratification. The thrill is gone. We must give them a hand by using reason and common sense to show them the way out of their moral crisis. We may not bring them to salvation, but we can influence them to live moral lives.

These moments of interaction with secular fellow employees and friends can do much to restore our culture to its Judeo-Christian roots. If the same principles and reasoning can also be brought into the media, classroom, politics, universities, and entertainment, then we will win the Culture War. We have to rethink how to speak to those in the secular world and know that we are not called only to bring salvation but also to bring influence. The majority will not be saved, since the way is narrow, but the majority can re-adopt the Judeo-Christian principles our nation followed since its beginnings. Once Americans see that these principles are true whether they are Christians or not, they can embrace them again. People are tired of the low culture our valueless society has created; they want out of the muck and violence caused by the socialist and humanist fabrications and falsehoods. The war is ours to win! It's time for us to use the weapon of the mind.

CHAPTER TEN

Calling Culture Warriors

Approximations

Winter's rebuke
and tumors of a dream
I once had--
sleep and...

BEHOLD!
The angle of them approaching
from endless arctic night,
their minds bursting with equations,
the storm whistles and cracks:
she is pregnant with their names.

BEHOLD!

Stumbling into view
they come closer
from a nightmare glow,
its Cartesian light carving a
silhouette of crescent moon smiles
on their shifting faces.

BEHOLD!
In Saturday hats and Sunday shoes
they have come
to pattern the earth red with plagues,
to paint the prophets' black,
to speak with hollow tongues,
to deceive with counterfeit love.

BEHOLD!
The trumpet sputters and coughs--
they have come
to a distance that has no reason
into a quantum state of not finding,
further from the closest star and closer
to a time…
when in a sleep not known,
yet, a new dream is tossed like a
seed from a framer's hand
into soil ready to receive it.
Sleep and….

(Valentino Vol, 2009)

"They have come to pattern the earth red with plagues, to paint the prophets black, to speak with hollow tongues, to deceive with counterfeit love." Yes, that is what we have been fighting for the last fifty years. Those who want to turn light into darkness and counterfeit Christ's principles with the Enemy's. Their minds have been "bursting with equations" to deceive and confuse Americans, and they have nearly succeeded. However, in spite of their progress, we have a covenant and prophecies that deny their victory. Just as they think they have won, God will pull our country back. "The trumpet sputters and coughs" and they fall into a "quantum state of not finding." Every trick and sleightofhand will fall flat. God will disperse their power in a moment. ". . . a new dream is tossed like a seed from the framer's hand into soil ready to receive it."

What is this new dream? The new dream is a dream revived. It's old but new. We understand now more than the Puritans did what were God's intentions. The opponents we face are more deceptive and dishonest than any enemy the Puritans could have imagined. The world was filled with deception then as well as now, for the Enemy is always the father of lies, but we battle against technology that creates a path into people's minds and hearts. We are fighting against tools of much greater power than previously.

However, those tools are our tools as well. Our soil is ready to receive the challenge. We can use the same technology to speak the truth and speak it even more exquisitely and perceptively than Satan. All that is needed are messengers—brave and dedicated messengers. I know many reading this book are called to be these messengers. Let God inspire and motivate you to join the army. The Puritans and Pilgrims knew they were God's soldiers, and they were prepared for and enthusiastic about fighting antichrists. Join God's armed forces; you won't be disappointed.

The prophet Edward Johnson enthusiastically expounded upon the importance of New England (America) in God's end time's plan:

> "Then judge all you (whom the Lord Christ hath given a discerning spirit) whether these poore New England People, be not the forerunners of Christs Army, and the marvelous providences which you shall now heare, be not the very Finger

of God, and whether the Lord hath not sent this people to Preach in this Wildernesse and to proclaime to all Nations, the neere approach of the most wonderfull workes that ever the Sonnes of men saw. Will not you believe that a Nation can be borne in a day? here is a worke come very neare it; but if you will believe you shall see far greater things than these, . . ."[1]

Reason or Emotion

The call to arms above is steeped in emotion, and emotion is appropriate when inspiring others to follow a dream. On the other hand, the actual battles and confrontations must be guided by reason. A major battle will involve fighting against the deceptive rationalism of President Obama. I have avoided focusing attention on Obama. But in reading his speech on religion, I understand the need to speak more specifically of his threat to restoring our nation to Judeo-Christian values.

In 2006, while still a senator, Obama gave a speech about religion entitled, "A Call to Renewal." It was a very rational speech, appealing to progressives and Christians to find a middle ground. I know he was very sincere in his evaluation of the issues that divide us, but if we succumb to his plea, we will have to accept a compromise that revolutionizes Christian morality.

The danger lies in reaching a compromise and a sense of proportion that creates a new morality, one that blends secularism and Christianity, thereby losing moral absolutes and Christian moral principles altogether because you cannot blend darkness and light without losing light. The following quotation reveals the compromising tone of his address: "And that is why that, if we truly hope to speak to people where they're at—to communicate our hopes and values in a way that's relevant to their own—then as progressives, we cannot abandon the field of religious discourse."[2]

In reading his speech, it's difficult to discern the irrational elements of his thinking. His arguments and requests appear rooted in reason and compromise. I am sure President Obama truly believed he was being very rational and moderate in requesting progressives and Christians to unite under the banners he constructed. He recognized the divisiveness of secular and religious disagreements and wanted civilized interaction. "Our failure as progressives to tap into the moral underpinnings of the nation is not just rhetorical, though. Our fear of getting "preachy" may also lead us to discount the role that values and culture play in some of our most urgent social problems. After all, the problems of poverty and racism, the uninsured, and the unemployed, are not simply technical problems in search of the perfect ten-point plan. They are rooted in both societal indifference and individual callousness—in the imperfections of man."[3]

The quote above expresses his thoughtful analysis of the problem. In fact, serious Christians should be able to make some headway under his administration in protecting some of the traditional Judeo-Christian practices in our nation. However, the greatest threat is for Christians to accept his thinking along with his recommendations. He has a definite flaw in his analysis of the role of Judeo-Christian principles in our nation's history and its present need for their application to our culture. One of those flaws is applying Christian principles to only poverty and racism. Progressives can agree with the black churches and social gospel traditions that racism and poverty are wrong and need to be corrected. Other Christians agree as well. The problem lies in making these the only issues (except stewardship of the earth has been added) to which you can apply Christian principles. You need to also apply Christian principles to the definitions of family, life, and freedom.

Another flaw in his thinking is revealed when he later mentioned particular Scriptures and applied them in a way that removed them from providing eternal principles on which we depend to guarantee our rights. He ridiculed the application of Deuteronomy, Leviticus, and the "turn the other cheek" of the Sermon on the Mount to modern problems. President Obama was unfamiliar with or ignored centuries of Christian scholarly and sophisticated interpretation of those Scriptures that make them understandable and relevant in modern times. He invalidated the practical application of the Bible by choosing aspects of it rather than turning to the centuries of tradition and wisdom built up through philosophical and theological analysis of Judeo-Christian principles as applied to the state and to the human condition. He opined, "Which passages of Scripture should guide our public policy? Should we go with Leviticus, which suggests slavery is okay and that eating shellfish is abomination? How about Deuteronomy, which suggests stoning your child if he strays from the faith? Or should we just stick to the Sermon on the Mount—a passage that is so radical that it's doubtful that our own Defense Department would survive its application? So before we get carried away, let's read our Bibles. Folks haven't been reading their Bibles."[4]

By mocking the inability to apply specific Scriptures to political problems, he ruled out the genuine contributions the Bible has provided. One of them is the guarantee of our inalienable rights because as stated in the Declaration of Independence, they come from the Creator. If he turned to Hinduism, Buddhism, or Islam, he would not derive the rights of man from their Scriptures, theological exegesis, or traditions. All religions cannot be thrown into the same pot of religious contributors to mankind as Christianity.

Since our Judeo-Christian God is the source of our rights, then that religious tradition has to provide and guide the application of those rights. Christian tradition provides the definition for life, family, charity, and liberty. It has always provided the guidelines for and description of our values and the formation of our government. By removing those guidelines, we are left with relativism, not the absolutes that guarantee our freedoms. As he so eloquently, but wrongly, declared, "Democracy demands that the religiously motivated translate their concerns into universal, rather than religion-specific, values. It requires that their proposals be subject to argument, and amenable to reason. I may be opposed to abortion for religious reasons, but if I seek to pass a law banning the practice, I cannot simply point to the teachings of my church or evoke God's will. I have to explain why abortion violates some principle that is accessible to people of all faiths, including those with no faith at all."[5]

How very reasonable he sounds! I can interpret his statement to mean abortion has nothing to do with when life begins, which has been decided by Judeo-Christian principles for two thousand years. Instead, it has to do with finding a common agreement with all members of a diverse society, finding common ground without using any moral absolutes to guide the decision. In just one half-hour speech, he managed to throw out two thousand years of Western, Judeo-Christian tradition.

Culture Warriors will have to be aware of these kinds of arguments to be able to refute and disarm them with rational, but true, statements. Even more important is the need to work traditional ideas back into the fabric of our society. Socialists have unrelentingly cut the threads holding our fabric together. We can mend the threads by seeking God's wisdom and truth as did our ancestors when they were sent to America. We can continue to follow their courageous example. They understood the need for loyalty to God and determined to fulfill His prophetic instructions.

Our Example

"The Lord will be our God, and delight to dwell among us, as His own people, and will command a blessing upon us in all our ways, so that we shall see much more of His wisdom, power, goodness and truth, than formerly we have been acquainted with."[6]

The passage above is drawn from the covenant John Winthrop wrote and the Puritans signed when they arrived in New England. It was called, "The Model of Christian Charity." The Puritans arrived on the *Arabella,* entered into a covenant with God and each other, and committed themselves to fulfilling their calling as Christians and as a new colony. They knew that God would reveal more of His plan to them as they obeyed Him. Their visions were not irrational and overenthusiastic dreams; they had received instructions through prophets in their midst. They came bearing instructions. It was not imagination gone wild or simplistic thinking. God originated the founding and settling of America. God required His American children to live morally and justly.

From the beginning our nation was called to practice justice and mercy and to be knit together as one. The Puritans believed God would punish them harshly if they failed to obey His calling: "Now the only way to avoid this shipwreck, and to provide for our posterity, is to follow the counsel of Micah, to do justly, to love mercy, to walk humbly with our God. For this end, we must be knit together, in this work, as one man."[7] The details of the calling were covered in chapter two. The most famous passage that has been a symbol and inspiration to America is: "For we must consider that we shall be as a City upon a Hill. The eyes of all people are upon us."[8] When measuring the success of our nation in fulfilling these instructions, we can see that we have much work ahead to restore those principles. It will take an American Restoration.

Restoration is necessary in order for America to fulfill another element of the original prophecy not yet covered. Edward Johnson referred to it in various places in his prophetic book. He revealed God's plan to use America to help restore Israel to its original status as God's chosen people and, as Paul predicted, that they would be grafted back into the Vine (Christ), as Paul described in Romans 11. The Puritans believed they were not only called to defend Israel and to be an example to make them jealous; they were also called to achieve the fullness for Gentile Christians that was required for the Jews to be restored to their place in the Vine.

If and when the New England Israel lived up to its calling as the City, it would also complete another of God's goals. In Ephesians 3, Paul explained the dispensation of grace God gave Him to bring the message of salvation to the Gentiles: "For this reason I, Paul, the prisoner of Christ Jesus for you Gentiles—if indeed you have heard of the dispensation of the grace of God which was given to me for you, . . . that the Gentiles should be fellow heirs, of the same body, and partakers of His promise in Christ through the gospel, of which I became a minister according to the gift of the grace of God given to me by the effective working of His power" (Eph. 3:1, 2, 6, 7).

In Romans 11, God used Paul to inform the Gentiles of their special place in God's plan, and how they were grafted into the Vine while the Jews were removed. However, he also had another message. Once the Gentiles reached their fullness, the Jews would be grafted back into the Vine. God revealed to the Puritans that

America had an instrumental role to play in achieving the "fullness of the Gentiles."

Johnson described the role of New England, which he referred to it as "low Shrubs" in contrast to the greater calling of Israel:

> "Finally, oh all yee Nations of the World, behold great is the worke the glorious King of Heaven and Earth hath in hand; beware of neglecting the call of Christ: and you the Seed of Israel both lesse and more, the ratling of your dead bones together is at hand, Sinewes, Flesh and Life: at the Word of Christ it comes. Counsellers and Judges you shall have as at the beginning to fight for you, as Gideon, Bareck, Jeptha, Samson etc. then sure your deliverance shall be sudden and wonderfull. If Christ have done such great things for these low Shrubs, what will his most Admirable, Excellent and wonderfull Worke for you be, but as the Resurrection from the dead, when all the miraculous acts of his wonderfull power shewed upon Pharoah for your fore-Fathers deliverance shall be swallowed up with those far greater workes that Christ shall shew for your deliverance upon the whole World, . . ."[9]

Johnson speaks of God using Israel for the "deliverance upon the whole World. . . ." However, as "low Sshrubs," the Puritans saw a special role for America as well. Isaiah 66 speaks of a nation born in a day. The Puritans believed that Scripture could be applied to New England as well as Israel. The New England Pilgrims and Puritans produced the fabric of our society with its main beliefs, purpose, vision, and ethical foundation. They were forerunners for God's future plan to prepare for His return. Their blueprint provided the elements needed to achieve the fullness of the Gentiles and accomplish its other callings as mentioned in chapter one.

It would fall to future generations of Americans, under the leadership and influence of Christians, to retain, strengthen, and develop that fabric. As our nation and its believers achieve that fullness and lead the way for Christians in other nations to do the same, God will continue in His plan to restore the Jews, fight antichrists, establish just governments, and purify the churches. Only the restoration of God's principles to our culture will guarantee the continuance of America's role in His plan.

The Reader's Role in Being an Agent of Restoration

I am certain God has called some churches to participate in America's restoration. I review some of the ideas in the next section to help pastors pursue this mission. I have also provided a Web site (www.winningtheculturewarthebook.com) to help in preparation, training, and coordination of our objectives. There are also groups of young people who are already trying to make changes in our culture, especially having to do with the life of the unborn. Any Christian group is welcome to join this movement. All those interested can contact me through my Web site. It would make it easier and more coordinated to have programs in churches for training and follow-up with small groups as a support. However, it may be difficult to draw pastors' attention away from their present visions and plans. If that is what occurs, then my Web site should be helpful for preparation, training, and coordination of our objectives.

If Saul Alinksy could train a small army of workers in Chicago, who over time had great influence in making socialism and secular humanism major forces in our culture, then *we* can do the same thing to restore Judeo-Christian principles to our culture. We have the advantage of having the Internet for strategy and training.

Christians in modern times always think big, but I want to think small. Small is good and small can become powerful. Look at the Puritans; they were "low Shrubs," and they changed the world. God always used the youngest, weakest, and smallest to accomplish His purposes—for example, David, Gideon, and Mary. We need only have a large passion. Culture Warriors must step forward. God has called certain people, some as regular soldiers and some as special forces. We are not alone and God needs us.

If you are an individual whose church is not involved, go to our Web site at www.winningtheculturewarthebook.com. You can join with other Culture Warriors online. The Left started with a few people entering universities, news media, movies, government, education, courts, and unions, and Satan was able to extend their influence into a Cultural Revolution. In addition, today, one of Alinsky's disciples is president of the United States. It only takes a few passionate and committed warriors. If your church doesn't offer a program of training for Culture Warriors, then join the Internet army. Welcome!

Churches' Role in Fulfilling God's Plans for America

We saw in chapter two the essential role of churches in God's plan for America. Churches provided the moral guidelines for the government. Governors of the colonies were expected to be as holy as if not holier than their pastors.

As mentioned in chapter three, the Founding Fathers believed that our democratic republic would fail if the people were not moral. That is why even the deists wanted Christian morality taught in the schools. Jefferson believed Jesus' moral teaching to be the highest form of morality the world had ever seen. He tried to follow Christ's teachings, although he didn't believe that Jesus was the Son of God.

Personal Experience

It was August 2002. I had won the Republican primary and was the Republican candidate for Congress in the fifteenth district of California. My campaign team was present and ready to be assigned their jobs. One of our strategies was to approach church pastors for an opportunity to speak at church services. According to federal law regulating the tax-exempt status of churches, I could be invited as long as the other candidate was invited as well. Normally, this other candidate didn't respond to those invitations from churches, so it would only require ten minutes during services on one Sunday.

We knew that if we could win over the Christians in the district that included parts of San Jose and Santa Clara, a very liberal area, we could go far in increasing my chances of winning. The redistricting of the Fifteenth District had given my opponent an added advantage, seeing that there was now an 11 percent margin of Democrats over Republicans instead of the original 7 percent advantage. However, if the Christian community could understand the issues and realize the conflict of their faith with my opponent's stand on social issues, I could at least organize a respectable challenge.

My husband began the calls to churches. He explained that I was a Christian and could assure my voting record would support Christian values. After many calls, no churches would allow me to speak. Later in the campaign through the intervention of various friends, two pastors allowed me to speak once in one of their services. Although most Christian pastors refused to let me speak, the Sikhs and Muslims set aside a time for me to make presentations. The Muslims actually organized a panel discussion including many different candidates.

The reason I give this above example is to reveal how out of touch most Christian churches and pastors are with the original relationship God established between church and state in our nation. Even after the spiritual inspiration for the abolitionist and civil rights movements, many Christian leaders have forgotten their role to accomplish God's ongoing plan for this nation. In modern times, many pastors have been manipulated into the politically correct thinking that religion has no place in politics. The institutions mentioned above, which deeply influence the minds of Americans, have done their job in the churches as well as the broader society. Many pastors feel uncomfortable informing their congregations of the moral contradictions they face when voting for the liberal members of either party. Pastors should guide their members when voting, not specifying the politicians but the standards by which to judge to various politicians. They should instruct their people that their representatives should represent their spiritual and moral values.

It's striking that many Christians separate their moral beliefs from the political arena. Many Christians—Protestants and Catholics—vote for candidates who are pro-choice, support homosexual marriage, and promote anti-Christian educational policies. How is this possible? How can Christians support a candidate who violates the moral teachings of Christ? Without a clear moral connection made between political policies and Christian faith, believers vote according to personal need or family tradition. They need to be taught their moral requirements when voting, to put righteousness before personal needs. Pastors should educate their members morally and invite candidates to explain their positions on issues and answer questions relating to their moral guidelines. James speaks of the "double-minded" person (James 1:8; 4:8). It's very possible for humans to hold two contradictory beliefs. Christians need help from those called to minister to them to discern the truth. People are not naturally logical; they have to be taught how to be morally logical and rational.

Since the 1960s our society has trusted in emotion more than reason. The hippie movement increased the influence of Romantic ideas introduced by Jean Jacques Rousseau in the eighteenth century. It was a rebellion against the rationalism of the Enlightenment period. The French Revolution was a bloody example of the result of uncontrolled passion and an over-enthusiastic faith in the goodness of the common man. America resisted many of the Romantic influences until the 1960s. At that time, it appealed to the liberal intellectuals because it provided ideas that supported a more secular and morally libertarian society.

The instability of much of our Christian community is the result of this secular, Romantic influence. Many Christians are struggling with emotional and mental instability. It's up to pastors to reintroduce the importance of reason and the power of reason over emotion. We need to reintroduce moral absolutes and define them. Believers should decide to do what is right because it's the right thing to do, not because something feels okay. Obedience and pleasing God must be a higher priority than following what feels right. The Bible clearly provides the teachings to order Christians' consciences. Somehow pastors need to get a handle on how to reeducate the consciences of their church family. It's difficult to balance God's justice with His mercy, not condemning yet teaching right behavior. Yet it must be done even at the threat of losing some members. Once the standard is set, the people will rise to meet it.

I mentioned earlier the pitfall for some pastors wanting to be a part of a broader elite group, more in agreement with the liberal society. I think some soul searching is required for pastors to ascertain if they have left behind the simple gospel of Christ crucified for a more sophisticated and socially acceptable message. The body of Christ needs to become more intellectual in order to impact society, but at the same time they must avoid becoming part of the intelligentsia. Warriors can embrace intellectual excellence in their education and careers while at the same time avoiding the elite snare.

Besides this tendency, there is one other area that hinders God's plan for our nation. Many churches don't recognize God's calling on some of their members to enter institutions that have been dominated by secular progressives. Most young people in the body of Christ unconsciously find themselves drawn into the institutions predetermined by the culture to be a fit for them. Most Christian youth are drawn to careers in the military, ministry, or business.

A teaching career is still popular for many Christian women, but they don't realize until they are hired by a public school that the teachers' unions have created a culture where Christian ideas are resisted. They are greatly restricted in having influence in their school district or in making policy for the school once they have been identified as Christians. They will not be invited to participate in union activities and decision making. Of course, they are very restricted and overly controlled in teaching any of America's Christian heritages in the classroom. It's one of the first areas to apply our new strategy. We will no longer yield to pressure but push forward in a firm but loving manner.

When I was teaching in a Christian high school, I noted that the majority of my students decide to choose marketing and business majors in college. I had some Christian students I knew would be exceptional journalists, lawyers, politicians, or university professors, but they avoided those fields for the less controversial ones. Some of them would have been willing to enter influential institutions if their pastors and parents had encouraged them. There are young believers right now who would feel more confident to enter secular institutions if pastors encouraged their youth of the importance of those callings and provided supporting ministries for them. Culture Warriors not only need to be encouraged to choose the careers in which they will experience greater conflicts and resistance, but they also need a place to come for prayer and guidance when they are tempted to yield to secular pressure. They should be praised and valued for their willingness to enter the mission field of secular institutions. Their calling is just as anointed and important as a ministry in the church. They are truly warriors, and their influence in these institutions will make the difference between our nation returning to its roots and letting secular progressives continue to dominate with their secular values.

Personal Experience

I mentioned earlier that, when I entered politics back in the late 1990s, the churches didn't accept me with open arms. I think cynicism was the obstacle. When I met with pastors, they treated me as if they were doing me a favor by letting me speak to their congregations. It didn't enter their minds that I was taking the hits in the secular trenches and that I was doing the body of Christ a favor by fighting a battle in the Culture War. I think they suspected my motives. They probably thought I wanted their support for my own self-interest of winning for the sake of winning. They didn't understand that I wanted to win to be able to reintroduce Judeo-Christian principles back into the culture.

I often felt more like an enemy than a friend. It made it difficult to believe that it was God's will for me to run for office. I was under the attack of shame from both sides. I also could have used more prayer support. If I had been able to attend meetings with other Christian candidates and been able to share my struggles, I could have been strengthened by their support and advice. It's the same for any warriors in every one of the institutions mentioned above. Christians are not betraying their faith by following God's calling into the secular battlefield. Intellectual and creative abilities are not reserved for use only in the body of Christ; they are part of God's arsenal to revolutionize the culture.

As mentioned in chapter six, I recommend that churches provide group meetings for Culture Warriors that focus on the issues these warriors face at work. They should be able to come and unload about their daily struggles and receive scriptural teachings and prayer to deepen their commitments.

The earlier chapters provided a guide for the kind of work the Lord will need to do in their hearts in order for them to remain committed and stay morally strong when approached with morally compromising decisions. Only by remaining steadfast in their dedication to upright behavior while being one of the best in their field will they be able to saturate the culture with godly ideas. Whether in the courts, filmmaking, universities, public schools, news or entertainment media, arts, or politics, they will reintroduce God's principles back into mainstream American society. Christians will be able to restore saltiness to their salt and be a light on a hill once more. They will help complete Paul's dispensation of grace that proclaimed and explained the special grace given to the Gentiles.

For a time, we saw some progress toward restoring traditional morality and principles to American society after the tragedy of 9/11. However, but these inroads have been difficult to sustain against the ongoing use of influential institutions to bombard Americans' hearts and minds with nontraditional, liberal values. Human nature is not good enough to resist promises of instant gratification. In other words, we cannot appeal to the moral sense or goodness within human nature to overcome the liberal, Cultural Revolution.

The institutions of a society mentioned above must be speaking with moral voices and from moral principles to sway minds and hearts to make moral choices. John F. Kennedy confirmed this truth about the importance of institutions in his "Strategy of Peace" speech in 1963. He stated we need a peace "based not on a sudden revolution in human nature but on a gradual evolution in human institutions."[10] The same principle applies to the reversal of the Cultural Revolution and establishing cultural peace in our nation. It's the changes in institutions not in human nature that will restore our culture to its earlier principles.

Edward Johnson proclaimed the miracle of America: "Will not you believe that a Nation can be borne in a day? here is a work come very near it; but if you will believe you shall see far greater things than these, and that in very little time, . . ."[11] And so he saw the fulfillment of Isaiah 66:7, 8 in the founding of America. Johnson and the Puritans believed God revealed to them that Isaiah was not only referring to Israel but also to God's "shrubs" in the wilderness of America. May the shrubs in our present wilderness answer the same prophetic appeal from God to keep alive His calling for this unique and anointed nation.

America has a job to finish. It still has to defeat antichrists, complete the fullness of the Gentiles to bring in the Jews, spread the Gospel, restore Judeo-Christian principles to our government and spread them to other oppressed nations, restore a desire for holiness, and return to its position as a City upon a Hill. Only we can make this happen. Only we can restore our nation to fulfill its prophetic calling. Maybe God will speak to us as He did to Columbus, the Puritans, and the abolitionists. If He spoke to our nation and the Christians in our nation, maybe He would say something like the following:

> You are my shrubs in the wilderness; you are little and not large. Yet you are special to me, for we have a covenant that will not be broken. Return to me and restore your callings that I imparted to you through my Puritan prophets. They are the root from which all of your purposes flow. Do not cut yourself off from the root. You are a nation created for a role in my greater plan. Do not ignore my calling, for to do so would mean destruction and death.
>
> You are mine and no other can have you. You are my tie to Israel, who is my sturdy tree under immense threat; you are her protector; you are her model; you are her salvation; she is your mother. Lay down your sins. They are an abomination to me. They grieve me beyond measure. Did I create my favored children to run riot in gratifying the flesh? Did I create my favored children so they could ignore my laws and replace

them with their own? Be holy as I am holy. No longer think you can postpone your obedience.

I wish to visit my people, but you have not let me. My shepherds cannot hear for their own imaginations absorb their minds. There is not room for the voice and instructions of my Spirit. Humble yourself and cry out for mercy. I am coming soon. Do not let me find you without oil in your lamps. Clean up your churches and restore my nation. No more games and glamour; no more self-importance. Don't forget you are a shrub, not a mighty tree. But, in spite of your faults, I adore you and love you and want to restore you to me. Let me visit you. Be silent! Be humble! Surrender your plans and receive your instructions from my Spirit.

NOTES

Chapter One

1. J. Edgar Hoover, *Masters of Deceit* (New York: Henry Holt and Company, 1958), 213.
2. Cleon W. Skousen, *The Naked Communist* (Salt Lake City: The Ensign Publishing Company 1962), 259–262.
3. John Perazzo, "Saul Alinsky" (5 April 2009), 12. http:/www. discoverthe networks.org/individualProfile.asp?indid=2314#_edn5 (accessed June 6, 2009).
4. Nik Richi, http://www.thedirty.com (accessed April 20, 2009).
5. Saul Alinsky, *Rules for Radicals* (New York: Vintage Books, 1989), 128.
6. Perazzo, 1.

Chapter Two

1. Christopher Columbus, *The Book of Prophecies Edited by Christoper Columbus, vol. 3* (Berkeley: University of California Press,1997), 67. The words in these quotations belong mainly to Columbus, but they are not direct quotations.
2. Ibid., 69.
3. Ibid., 67.
4. Ibid.
5. Ibid., 75.
6. Ibid., 59.
7. Kevin Miller, "Why Did Columbus Sail?" *Christian History* (July 1, 1992), http://www.millersville.edu/ (accessed December 2, 2009).
8. Ibid., 1.
9. Ibid.
10. Ibid.
11. Ibid.

12. Bill Gothard, "Understanding Rhema," 1. http://billgothard.com/bill/ teach ing/rhemas/(accessed January 25, 2009).

13. Edward Johnson, *Wonder-Working Providence of Sions Saviour in New England (Delmar, NY: Scholars Facsimiles & Reprints, 1974)*, 23.

14. Ibid.

15. Johnson, 23.

16. Ibid., 2.

17. Ibid.

18. Ibid., 7.

19. Ibid., 181.

20. Ibid., 233.

21. Ibid., 7.

22. Sacvan Bercovitch, *The Puritan Origins of the American Self* (London: Yale University Press, 1975), 61.

23. Johnson, 7.

24. John Calvin, http://www.iclnet.org/pub/ resources/text/ipb-e/epl-09/cvin 4 22.txt (accessed June 20,2007)

25. Johnson, 7.

26. Ibid., 233.

27. Perry Miller, *The Puritans* (New York: Harper Torchbooks, 1963), 194.

28. Bercovitch, 92.

Chapter Three

1. Josiah Benjamin Richards, ed., *God of Our Fathers* (Reading: Reading Books, 1994), 190.

2. Johnson, 3.

3. Richards, 190.

4. Page Smith, *The Constitution* (New York: Morrow Quill Paperbacks, 1980), 40.

5. James Madison, *Federalist Papers, No. 51,* http://www.foundingfathers.info/ federalistpapers/fed.htm (accessed June 13, 2009). http://www.constitution.org/ fed/federa51.htm.

6. Smith, 93.

7. Ibid., 54, 55.

8. Ibid., 95.

9. Ibid., 145.

10. Ibid., 100.

11. Ibid., 148.

12. Ibid., 151.

13. Ibid., 158.

14. Ibid., 162.

15. Ibid.

16. Johnson, 3.

17. Smith, 174.

18. Ibid., 173.

19. Ibid., 176.

20. Ibid., 177.

21. Ibid., 178.

22. Ibid., 181.

23. Ibid., 225–26.

24. Ibid., 229–30.

25. James Madison, *Federalist Papers, No. 37.* http://www.foundingfathers .info/federalistpapers/fed.htm (accessed June 13, 2009).

Chapter Four

1. Johnson, 7.

2. Johnson, 7.

3. William Lloyd Garrison, "To the Public," from *The Liberator,* January 1861), http://www.pbs.org/wgbh/aia/part4/4h2928t.html (accessed May 10. 2008).

4. Douglas M. Strong, *Perfectionist Politics* (New York: Syracuse University Press, 1999), 81.

5. Joel Tiffany, *A Treatise on the Unconstitutionality of American Slavery: Together With the Powers and Duties of the Federal Government in Relation to That Subject* (Cleveland: J. Calyer, 1849), 55, http://medicolegal.tripod.com/ tiffanyuos. htm#p55-preamble (accessed May 11, 2008).

6. Lysander Spooner, *Unconstitutionality of Slavery* (Boston: Bela Marsh, 1845, 3rd ed., 1860), 123–24. http://medicolegal.tripod.com/spooneruos. htm#preamble-p90 (accessed May 12, 2008).

7. Rev. John G. Fee, *An Anti-Slavery Manual, or, The Wrongs of American Slavery Exposed By the Light of the Bible and of Facts, with A Remedy for the Evil,* 2d ed. (New York: William Harned, 1851) 124, http://medicolegal.tripod. com/ feeasm1851.htm (accessed May 12, 2008).

8. Angelina Grimké Weld's speech at Pennsylvania Hall, *History of Pennsylvania Hall which was Destroyed by a Mob on the 17th of May, 1838,* (New York: Negro Universities Press, A Division of Greenwood Publishing Corp, 1969), http:// www.pbs.org/wgbh/aia/part4/4h2939t.html (accessed May 17, 2008).

9. Frederick Douglass's lecture, "Unconstitutionality of Slavery," March 26, 1860, 15, 16. http://medicolegal.tripod.com/douglassuos.htm (accessed May 12, 2008)

10. Alvan Stewart, 21–22 May 1845 speech to the New Jersey Supreme Court, "Legal Argument For the Deliverance of Persons from Bondage," 46. http://medico legal.tripod.com/stewartuos.htm#p46-constitution-anti-slavery (accessed May 17, 2008).

11. Abraham Lincoln, Speech at Peoria, Illinois, The Lincoln Log, (16 October 1854), CW, 2:247–83. 255, http://www.thelincolnlog.org/view/1854/10/16 (accessed May 17, 2008).

12. Johnson, 6.

13. Lincoln/Douglas Debate, 276.

14. Ibid., 256.

15. Ibid., 275.

16. Abraham Lincoln, Speech, "Our Reliance Is in the Love of Liberty," Edwardville, Illinois, (11 September 1858), 128. http://books.google.com/ boo

ks?id=8bWmmyJEMZoC&pg=PA127&lpg=PA127&dq=our+reliance+is+in
+the+love+of+liberty&source=bl&ots=vEeuxiQjmv&sig=J7loIkMFTo7_QYru
-wX5XrXYv_s&hl=en&ei=UpJwSpWHCoeOtAP__sTHCA&sa=X&oi=book_result
&ct=result&resnum=1 (accessed May 21, 2008).
17. Abraham Lincoln, "A letter to Albert G. Hodges," (4 April 1864). http://
showcase.netins.net/web/creative/lincoln/speeches/hodges.htm (accessed May 21,
2008).

Chapter Five

1. Johnson, 7.
2. Ibid., 233.
3. Adolf Hitler, *Mein Kampf,* Chapter 11, "Nation and Race,"(July, 1925)
http://www.hitler.org/writings/Mein_Kampf/mkv1ch11.html (accessed August 1,
2008).
4. Ibid.
5. Ibid.
6. Ibid.
7. D. Sklar, *The Nazis and the Occult,* (New York: Dorset Press, 1977), 146.
This book has quotations based on an interview that has not been corroborated. I
used the information for effect not for its accuracy. This thought doesn't break from
Hitler's ideas in Mein Kampf.
8. Martin Luther King, Jr., "I See the Promised Land," 13 April 1968, http://
www.mlkonline.net/promised.html (accessed August 20, 2008).
9. Martin Luther King, Jr., "Speech at the Great March in Detroit," 23 June
1963, http://www.mlkonline.net/detroit.html (accessed August 20, 2008).
10. Henry M. Morris, "Ideas Have Consequences," *Acts and Facts* (June 2009), 22.

Chapter Six

1. Cleon W. Skousen, *The Naked Communist* (Salt Lake City: The Ensign
Publishing Company, 1962), 261.
2. William W. Sweet, *The Story of Religion in America* (Grand Rapids: Baker
Book House, 1979), 356.
3. Nancy Pearcy, *Total Truth* (Orange, CA: Crossway Books, 2004), 281.
4. Ibid.
5. Pope John Paul II, *Evangelium Vitae,* (25 March 1995), http://www.vatican
.va/edocs/ENG0141/_INDEX.HTM (June 10, 2009).

Chapter Seven

1. Bernard Goldberg, *100 People Who Are Screwing Up America* (New York:
Harper Collins Publishers, 2005), 304.

Chapter Eight

1. Saul Alinsky, *Rules for Radicals: A Practical Primer for Realistic Radicals* (New York: Vintage Books 1971), 24.
2. Ibid., 125.
3. Ibid., 137.
4. Ibid., 130.
5. Ibid., 7.
6. Ibid., 134.
7. Ibid., 125.
8. Ibid., 136.
9. Suzanne Adelson, "Comedy Writer Doug Gamble Gives a Lift to the G.O.P., and Vice Versa," (7 December 1984), http://www.douggamble.com/clips.htm (accessed June 30, 2009).
10. Alinsky, 129.
11. Ibid.
12. Ibid., 33.

Chapter Nine

1. J. P. Moreland, Love Your God with All Your Mind (Colorado Springs: Navpress, 1997), 25.
2. Ibid., 26.
3. Jeremiah Films, "Experiment with Socialism, Socialism gets an F." http://www.jeremiahfilms.com/released/WhiteHouse/SeedsOfSocialism/903251815 (accessed July 2, 2009).
4. Discovery Institute—Center for Science and Culture, http://www.intelligentdesign.org/whatisid.php (accessed July 2, 2009).
5. Dennis Prager, "The Case for Judeo-Christian Values: Part II (11 January 2005), http://townhall.com/columnists/DennisPrager/2005/01/11/the_case_for_judeo-christian_values_part_ii (accessed July 2, 2009).
6. G. K. Chesterton, http://chesterton.org/qmeister2/any-everything.htm (accessed July 21, 2009). This quote is credited to Chesterton, but it's not a certainty that he said (or wrote) it.

Chapter Ten

1. Johnson, 34.
2. Barack Obama, "Call to Renewal Keynote Address," 28 June 2006, http://www.barackobama.com/2006/06/28/call_to_renewal_keynote_address.php (accessed July 29, 2009).
3. Ibid.
4. Ibid.
5. Ibid.
6. Perry Miller and Thomas H. Johnson, *The Puritans, vol.1* (New York: Harper & Row, 1963), 198.
7. Ibid.
8. Ibid., 199.

9. Johnson, 33.

10. John F. Kennedy, "Strategy of Peace," speech (10 June 1963), http://www.fordham.edu/halsall/mod/1963kennedy-peacestrat.html (accessed January 3, 2008).

11. Johnson, 34.

WORKS CITED

Adelson, Suzanne. "Doug Gamble Writer." http://www.douggamble
.com/clips.htm (accessed June 30, 2009).

Chesterton, G. K. "Quotemeister." *The American Chesteron Society.*
http://chesterton.org/qmeister2/any-everything.htm (accessed
July 21, 2009).

Douglas, Fredrick. Fredrick Douglas's lecture, "Unconstitutionality
of Slavery." *The History of Abolitionism in America.* March 26,
1860. http://medicolegal.tripod.com/douglassuos.htm (accessed
May 12, 2008).

Fee, Rev. John G. "The History of Abolitionism in the United
States." *The Wrongs of American Slavery Exposed by the Light
of the Bible and of Facts.* 1851. http://medicolegal.tripod.com/
feeasm1851.htm (accessed May 12, 2008).

Garrison, William Lloyd. "Africans in America." PBS. January 1,
1831. http://www.pbs.org/wgbh/aia/part4/4h2928t.html (accessed
May 10, 2008).

Goldberg, Bernard. *100 People Who Are Screwing Up America.*
New York: Harper Collins Publishers, 2005.

Hitler, Adolf. "Nation and Race." *Mein Kampf.* July 1925. http://
www.hitler.org/writings/Mein_Kampf/mkv1ch11.html
(accessed August 1, 2008).

Well of Oath. "Bio's: Reese Howell 1879–1950." http://www.well ofoath.com/home.asp?pg=Newsletter&toc=November+2004 (accessed July 29, 2009).

John Paul II. "Evangelium Vitae." *Holy See-The Holy Father.* March 25, 1995. http://www.vatican.va/edocs/ENG0141/_INDEX.HTM (accessed June 10, 2009).

Intelligentdesign.org. *Center for Science and Culture.* 2009. http://www.intelligentdesign.org/whatisid.php (accessed July 2, 2009).

Kennedy, John F. "John F. Kennedy: Towards a Strategy of Peace." *Modern History Sourcebook.* June 10, 1963. http://www.fordham.edu/halsall/mod/1963kennedy-peacestrat.html (accessed January 3, 2008).

King, Martin Luther, Jr. "I See the Promised Land." *MLK Online.* April 13, 1968. http://www.mlkonline.net/promised.html (accessed August 20, 2008).

———. "Martin Luther King Speeches." *MLK Online.* August 28, 1963. http://www.mlkonline.net/dream.html (accessed August 20, 2008).

———. "Speech on the Great March on Detroit." *MLK Online.* June 23, 1963. http://www.mlkonline.net/detroit.html (accessed August 20, 2008).

Lincoln, Abraham. "Collected Works of Abraham Lincoln." *The Lincoln Log.* October 16, 1854. http://www.thelincolnlog.org/view/1854/10/16 (accessed May 17, 2008).

———. "Letter to Albert G. Hodges." *Abraham Lincoln Online.* April 4, 1864. http://showcase.netins.net/web/creative/lincoln/speeches/hodges.htm (accessed May 21, 2008).

———. "Lincoln on Democracy." *Google Books.* September 11, 1858. http://books.google.com/books?id=8bWmmyJEMZoC&pg=PA127&lpg=PA127&dq=our+reliance+is+in+the+love+of+liberty&source=bl&ots=vEeuxiQjmv&sig=J7loIkMFTo7_QYru-wX5XrXYv_s&hl=en&ei=UpJwSpWHCoeOtAP__sTHCA&sa=X&oi=book_result&ct=result&resnum=1 (accessed May 21, 2008).

Moreland, J. P. *Love Your God with All Your Mind.* Colorado Springs: Navpress, 1997.

Morris, Henry M. "Ideas Have Consequences." *Acts & Facts,* June 2009: 22.

Obama, Barack. "Call to Renewal Keynote Address." *Organizing for America.* June 28, 2006. http://www.barackobama.com/2006/06/28/call_to_renewal_keynote_address.php (accessed June 25, 2009).

Pearcy, Nancy. *Total Truth.* Orange, CA: Crossway Books, 2004.

Sklar, D. *The Nazis and the Occult.* New York: Dorset Press, 1977.

Obama Seeds of Socialism: "Experiment with Socialism, Socialism Gets an F." *Jeremiah Films.* 2009. *(accessed July 2, 2009).*

Spooner, Lysander. "History of Abolitionism in the United States." *Unconstitutionality of Slavery* . 1860. http://medicolegal.tripod.com/spooneruos.htm#preamble-p90 (accessed May 12, 2008).

Stewart, Alvan. "Legal Argument for the Deliverance of Persons from Bondage." *History of Abolitionism in the United States.* May 21-22, 1845. http://medicolegal.tripod.com/stewartuos.htm#p46-constitution-anti-slavery. (accessed May 17, 2008).

Strong, Douglas M. *Perfectionist Politics.* Syracuse, NY: Syracuse University Press, 1999.

Sweet, William W. *The Story of Religion in America.* Grand Rapids, MI: Baker Book House, 1979.

Tiffany, Joel. "A Treatise on the Unconstitutionality of American Slavery." *History of Abolitionism in the United States.* 1849. http://medicolegal.tripod.com/tiffanyuos.htm#p55-preamble (accessed May 11, 2008).

Weld, Angelina Grimke. "Africans in America." PBS. May 17, 1838. http://www.pbs.org/wgbh/aia/part4/4h2939t.html (accessed May 14, 2009).

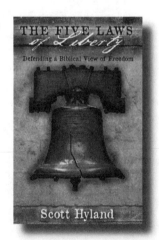

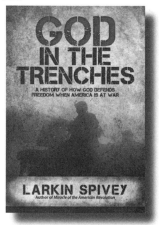

OTHER BOOKS FROM GOD AND COUNTRY PRESS

DEATH OF A CHRISTIAN NATION

DEBORAH DEWART

ISBN-13: 978-0-89957-023-5

THE FIVE LAWS OF LIBERTY: DEFENDING A BIBLICAL VIEW OF FREEDOM

SCOTT HYLAND

ISBN-13: 978-0-89957-015-0

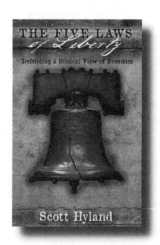

FOR MORE INFORMATION VISIT

WWW.GODANDCOUNTRYPRESS.COM

OR CALL 800-266-4977

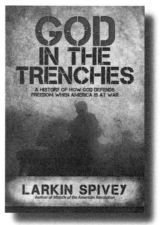